Discover Missouri's State Parks

MISSOURI'S IDENTITY HAS LONG BEEN TIED to its role as a crossroads, a land—sometimes a battleground—where east met west, and south confronted north. This borderland character has produced extraordinary personalities and enduring human stories. The same crossroads geography also shapes the state's landscapes and environment, from the rich rolling plains of the north and west, through the ancient wooded Ozark hills and hollows to the broad alluvial delta of the deep southeast, and along the corridors of the continent's two mightiest rivers.

The state's remarkable diversity of people and resources comes alive in this updated second edition of this guide that explores all there is to see and do in our superb state park system. Taum Sauk, Onondaga, and Ha Ha Tonka are here, all about Ozark mountains, caves, and springs. Mastodon State Historic Site, saved only by the refusal of four housewives to take "no" for an answer, revealed the first proof of humans in contact with mastodons 12,000 years ago, while Watkins Mill showcases a farm that added a factory and became a National Historic Landmark.

Big Lake, Big Oak Tree, and Confluence ponder the lessons of our restless big rivers, while Pershing Park in the north and Prairie in the southwest exhibit fascinating stories of landscapes restored by park staff. More than a score of historic sites honor consequential Missourians—Osage Village and Towosahgy, but also Harry S. Truman, Mark Twain, and Scott Joplin. Other parks and sites preserve Civil War battlefields, ridges, mills, mines, reservoirs, and trails, each with a powerful story to tell.

Short essays for each of Missouri's parks and historic sites treat them with insight into each place's main attractions and what makes them special, and beautiful color photographs illuminate each place. Whether packed in your backpack or resting on your nightstand, this volume will serve you as a comprehensive guide to Missouri's park system.

Missouri has one of the best state park systems in the country, and this guide is the most up-to-date you will find on our state parks. Most of all, we offer this guide to readers in Missouri everywhere as an evergreen source of inspiration to get out and explore the Show-Me State's great outdoors and historic sites. We invite you to discover the best of Missouri!

Cover photo: Mina Sauk Falls at Taum Sauk Mountain State Park. *Glenn Curcio*

A mountain biker enjoys the new Kelley Branch trail at Finger Lakes State Park. Local volunteers helped build the trail. *Ben Nickelson* Children love to play on the elephants at Elephant Rocks State Park. The ancient pink granite boulders dominate the park. *Scott Myers*.

Let us be your guide!

From prairie vistas to Ozark mountain forests to lakeside views, these drives have something for everyone, often on the same route. So pick one, and hit the road. In Missouri, there's always more to discover. *48 pages, $5, softcover*

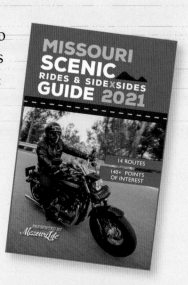

No other immigrant group has had a greater influence on Missouri than the Germans.

This book is your personal tour guide into that unique heritage. It includes rare archival materials as well as places you can visit today to help you explore that history or sample their culture. *164 pages, $34.99, softcover*

THE SPIRIT OF DISCOVERY

VISIT MISSOURILIFE.COM/SHOP OR CALL TOLL-FREE 1-877-570-9898 TO ORDER YOURS TODAY!

Missouri State Parks

Discover all 92 Parks

Missouri Parks Association graciously granted permission to use the book, "Missouri State Parks and Historic Sites, Exploring our Legacy," (second edition), edited by Susan Flader, and written by Susan Flader, John Karel, and B. H. Rucker, with photography by Oliver Schuchard and others, which was jointly published by Missouri Life, Inc., and Missouri Parks Association, as the primary source of information. Words and photographs are used with permission. Missouri State Parks also assisted with verifying information.

MissouriLife
THE SPIRIT OF DISCOVERY

208 Columbia Street, Rocheport, MO 65279
573-514-5453 | Info@MissouriLife.com

Publisher Greg Wood
Editor in Chief Danita Allen Wood

EDITORIAL & ART
Special Projects Editor & Manager Rebecca French Smith
Creative Director Holly Kite
Graphic Designers Kath Teoli, Dan Bishop

MARKETING • 877-570-9898
Advertising & Marketing Director
Deborah Marshall, 573-514-5453

Marketing and Advertising Coordinator
Amy Stapleton, 573-514-5453

Share your state parks adventures with us and discover more with Missouri Life magazine!

FIND US ONLINE OR SOCIAL MEDIA
Search for Missouri Life Magazine on Facebook to send us a message, or tweet us @MissouriLife. Share pictures with us on Instagram @MissouriLifeMag.

HOW TO REACH US
SUBSCRIPTION INFORMATION:
MissouriLife.com
missourilife@emailcustomerservice.com
1-800-492-2593

ALL OTHER INFORMATION: 1-877-570-9898
info@missourilife.com
Missouri Life, 208 Columbia Street, PO Box 57, Rocheport, MO 65279

Contents & Park Locations

 Camping

 Fishing

 Hiking trails

 Biking trails

 Equestrian trails

 Dining

 Picnic area

 Lodging

 Swimming

 Boating

 Playground

 Floating/Kayaking

 Orienteering

 Rock climbing

 Off roading

 Information: visitor center, interpretive programs, or site tours

 Guided Cave Tours

HOW TO USE THIS GUIDE

This guide devotes one page to each of Missouri's 92 state parks and historic sites, featuring beautiful images, detailed descriptions, and quick facts to help you navigate each location. On the outside margin of each page is a stack of icons depicting various park amenities. Icons highlighted red indicate the activity is available at the park; gray means it is not. Walking, biking, hiking, and horse riding trails are listed on each page, along with a map showing the park's location within the state, the county, and park acreage.

We created this guide to serve you as you explore Missouri—take it with you on your next trip and you'll never be far from adventure!

Map Key
● State park
■ Historic site

Missouri River

Katy Trail

Mississippi River

Arrow Rock State Historic Site

39521 Visitor Center Dr, Arrow Rock

Arrow Rock appeared on maps as early as 1732. It takes its name from a flinty river bluff that Native Americans used as a place to make flint tools and weapons.

167 acres
Saline County

Trails
- Pierre a Flèche Trail (1.5 mi)
- River Landing Trail (0.3 mi)

AS THE STATE'S FIRST HISTORIC SITE, Arrow Rock holds a place of honor in the state park system. Today, as in the past, it beckons to travelers passing through the Missouri River valley. The Missouri River was and is the dominant geographic feature of the region, and an important Indian trail known as the Osage Trace crossed the Missouri River here.

The site was noted by Lewis and Clark on their expedition upriver in 1804 and again in 1808 by William Clark, who deemed it "a handsome Spot for a Town." Small enclaves of American pioneers settled in the region by 1810.

After the War of 1812, settlers flooded into the area "like an avalanche," said Baptist missionary John Mason Peck. In September 1821, a party under William Becknell crossed on the Arrow Rock ferry and followed the Osage Trace on what became the first successful trading venture to Santa Fe.

An exceptional visitor center and museum contain exhibits on the Osage and Missouria tribes, the French and Spanish time here, and on American pioneers. The home of artist George Caleb Bingham is a favorite on tours, and the Friends of Arrow Rock, Inc. have restored the 1869 Brown's Chapel Free Will Baptist Church and the 1881 Brown Lodge (Black Masonic Lodge), now a museum showcasing the black culture of the town. A nearly 2,000-acre federal wildlife refuge borders the site, and walking trails connect to it. *

Top: Arrow Rock's quiet, shady streets even today evoke the nineteenth century. The Friends of Arrow Rock now maintain the Masonic and Odd Fellows lodge halls, which face each other across Main Street. *Friends of Arrow Rock* • Middle: Many special events take visitors back to different eras, along a boardwalk and street lined with shops built in the nineteenth century. *Mike Kellner* Bottom: The Huston Tavern has accommodated western travelers since the 1830s and still serves hearty fare to its guests. *Missouri State Parks*

Dr. Edmund A. Babler Memorial State Park

800 Guy Park Dr, Wildwood

BABLER STATE PARK IS SPECIAL for many reasons: its origin, its funding, its facilities, its rich botanical diversity, and its location in St. Louis County on the fringe of Missouri's largest metropolitan area. The Dr. Edmund A. Babler Memorial State Park is one of the most heavily visited parks in the system. When it was dedicated in 1938, the park was a long drive into the country. Now, it is an open-space oasis amid a rapidly expanding suburban landscape.

The park was given to the state as a living memorial for St. Louis physician Edmund A. Babler by his two brothers, Jacob and Henry. Their father, Henry J. Babler settled in Eldorado Springs, Missouri, in the 1870s. The family prospered in Missouri, with all three brothers establishing themselves as leaders in St. Louis by the early twentieth century. Edmund had a stroke and caught pneumonia and died at age fifty-four.

Jacob and Henry donated the first tract of 868 acres to the state in 1934 and added nearly 800 acres more within two years. The state has acquired some additional tracts, bringing the total to nearly 2,500 acres.

The mid-1930s were the years of New Deal-sponsored work relief in the parks, and a substantial allocation of labor to develop the park came from the Civilian Conservation Corps (CCC) along with the Works Progress Administration (WPA)—more than for any other park in Missouri. The elaborate twenty-two structures from the CCC era, including the stone lodge, are now part of the Babler historic district on the National Register of Historic Places.

The evidence suggests that Jacob Babler took a decidedly proprietary interest in the park, visiting the CCC crews at work there almost daily, meeting with the park's designer, commissioning a noted New York sculptor to create a statue of his brother, and traveling to Washington, DC, to discuss plans with National Park Service staff.

The park that Babler built is a fascinating mix of urban and rural. The massive stone gateway, the entry avenue wider than a city boulevard with stone gutters and curbing, the manicured landscaping against a forest backdrop, the life-sized bronze statue of Dr. Edmund Babler—all are evocative of great urban parks.

Babler Park reflects the shared vision of St. Louis planners and civic leaders of a great outer loop of parks interconnected by parkways. One of the special distinctions of Babler Park is the Jacob L. Babler

The park represents a classic Ozark Border landscape: rugged, rocky hills and ridges. Massive oaks and these magnificent hawthorn maples grace northern and eastern slopes and ravines. *Missouri State Parks*

Outdoor Education Center, a barrier-free group camp. Park staff also run one-day summer camp experiences called Babler Outdoor Adventure for school-aged children.

The CCC-era stable no longer houses an equestrian concession but instead is used by Rockwood School District as an outpost for Babler Wild, a series of week-long summer camps. An impressive visitor center completed in 1991 houses special exhibits about the natural history of the park.

High quality natural features immediately adjacent to the St. Louis metropolitan area coupled with classic park design and distinctive recreational opportunities make this a true gem of the state park system, thanks to the splendid vision of the Babler brothers. *

2,441 acres
St. Louis County

Trails
- Dogwood Trail (2 mi)
- Equestrian Trail (6 mi)
- Hawthorn Trail (1.25 mi)
- Paved Bicycle Path (1.75 mi)
- Virginia Day Memorial Nature Trail (1.5 mi)
- Woodbine Trail (2 mi)

Historic Structures
- CCC stone lodge and other structures

Life was hard in rural Wayne County where Sam A. Baker was born, grew up, and later taught school. After a career in education, Baker was elected governor of Missouri in 1924. During his term, many of the first-generation of state parks were acquired—not least of them the forested, mountainous tract of canyons, shut-ins, and rushing streams in Wayne County, close to the village of Patterson where the governor was born.

5,324 acres
Wayne County

Trails
- Fire Tower Trail (2 mi)
- Mudlick Trail (3 trail options from 5.5 to 16.75 mi)
- Paved Bicycle Trail (1.5 mi)
- Shut-Ins Trail (1.25 mi)

Historic Structures
- CCC bridges, cabins, trail shelters, and more.
- WPA dining lodge

Sam A. Baker State Park

Rt 1, Patterson

ON THE SOUTHERN FLANK of the St. Francois Mountains, Sam A. Baker offers visitors the freedom to wander at will in spacious, wild lands, savor old-time park hospitality in rustic comfort, enjoy the refreshing tingle of a clear Ozark mountain stream, and ascend the blue granitic hulk of Mudlick Mountain, where you can survey virtually the entire panorama of the St. Francois Mountains and scan the deeply dissected hills of the Ozark border that drops off into the Mississippi Lowlands beyond.

This classic Missouri state park stands out in bold relief, encompassing all of Mudlick Mountain and the adjacent streams. On the east side, the park fronts on the St. Francis River and for about five miles on its tributary, Big Creek. Huge boulders of Precambrian Mudlick dellenite, called blue granite by the locals, litter the hillsides and canyons. Rushing creek waters polish them to a beautiful sheen.

Because the park was established under the old Missouri Game and Fish Commission, a large portion of the mountainous area was initially set aside as a big-game refuge. Today, deer and wild turkey have returned to their former abundance, both inside the park and in the state, and no longer require artificial measures for their propagation.

Cultural as well as natural resources make this park a Missouri classic. The first major construction came when the park became the site of Civilian Conservation Corps (CCC) Camp 5, set up in 1933 in the valley near the present-day visitor center. By 1935, CCC enrollees had built barracks, installed telephone and water lines, laid out trails, planted trees, fought fires, and built a number of well-crafted rustic structures, including bridges, cabins, barbecue pits, restrooms, trail shelters, a gatekeeper's stand, and a stable. Works Progress Administration (WPA) workers completed a timber and blue granite dining lodge.

These handsome, sturdy, Depression-era structures continue to function in the park today. Indeed, they set the tone for the park. Owing to the integrity of the preserved CCC and WPA workmanship, the 4,860 acres of the 1930s park have been designated on the National Register of Historic Places.

The park offers Missourians an authentic Ozark experience with six trails for hiking, biking, or horse riding, and hands-on nature exhibits. *

Top: Mudlick Creek, a beautiful Ozark stream, gurgles through a rocky hollow in the Mudlick Mountain Wild Area. *Michelle Soenksen* • Middle: A park naturalist—or else the snake—entrances children. • Bottom: Riders enjoy seventeen miles of equestrian trails. *Both Scott Myers*

Battle of Athens State Historic Site

Rt CC, Revere

A BATTLE RAGED between strong-willed and passionate partisan Missourians in Clark County on August 5, 1861. It was one of the earliest skirmishes and perhaps the farthest north of the Civil War. When the smoke cleared, there were a few dozen casualties and the pro-South forces were in retreat, but the big loser was the town, where bitter feelings remained long after the war.

One hundred years after the battle, the Athens Park Development Association organized and began purchasing land to commemorate the battle, an idea that had been promoted ever since 1900 when local residents held the first of a nearly annual series of August 5 celebrations. The new association wanted the state to develop the property, but the Missouri State Park Board demurred on the grounds that the site did not have high priority for preservation. Undaunted, the association continued to acquire tracts, financed with the proceeds from motorcycle hill climbs it staged annually up a steep embankment along the river.

It was not until 1975 that the state accepted the 235-acre donation, and then as a park rather than a historic site. With a 10-acre lake for swimming, excellent fishing on the river, and a good place for a campground, the property could provide much-needed recreation facilities in a corner of the state relatively deficient in public lands. Then in 1981, in the course of an archaeological survey for a waterline across the park to the new campground, several discoveries changed the perception of the area. Ar-

A cannonball ripped through the Thome-Benning home at this historic site. The restoration of the home preserved the original hole right next to the kitchen door, earning the home the name "the cannonball house."

409 acres
Clark County

Trails

- Mill Trail (0.3 mi)
- Snow Trillium Trail (2 mi)

chaeologists found a number of prehistoric Indian sites and part of a large historic Sauk Indian village that had been occupied as late as the 1830s. They also found evidence of nearly the entire site of Athens as laid out in 1844 by Isaac Gray in nine blocks of eight lots each. Still standing were the Smith Hotel and three houses, but of the fifty or so businesses operating before the Civil War, little remained except for the stone foundation of the grist, saw, and woolen mill down by the river.

With a wealth of structural remains and substantial archaeological and archival potential, park officials in 1985 decided to reclassify Battle of Athens as a historic site and began an ambitious research and development plan that has brought the site to more than 400 acres.

Archaeology has now exposed old foundations and roads, which are being stabilized, slightly reconstructed, or outlined on the ground for guiding visitors on a full-size map of the town.

State park naturalists identified outstanding and unique natural features in the forested ravines along the Des Moines River northwest of the town. The ravines adjoin an upland area of former glacial-loess prairie being restored to reveal an unusually tight transition from open prairies to oak woodland to dense forest to riparian cottonwoods, a combination that surely attracted the Sauk and other native peoples as well as white settlers. A forty-acre site, protected as the Des Moines River Ravines Natural Area, is accessible via a two-mile loop trail.

The Civil War is still vitally important here, and we can explore the war's impact on ordinary people caught in a vortex of change in this seemingly ordinary little river town. ✶

Left: The park shelters a rich flora that includes snow trillium (shown) and doll's eyes, relics of glacial times. *Bruce Schuette* • Right: The brick house was built around 1857 by Southern sympathizer William Moreland, who was taken prisoner during the battle. *Jerry Toops*

Battle of Carthage State Historic Site

E Chestnut St, Carthage

More Missourians fought in the Civil War, in proportion to the state's population, than was the case in any other state. Some 60 percent of eligible men saw action—at least 50,000 served the Confederacy and 109,000 the Union. More than 8,000 black Missourians enlisted in Missouri regiments. About 14,000 Missourians gave their lives for the Union, and even more for the Confederacy.

**7 acres
Jasper County**

ONE OF THE EARLIEST ENGAGEMENTS of the Civil War, the Battle of Carthage preceded the Battle of Bull Run by eleven days. This site marks one of the last skirmishes of the battle and the place where both opponents camped, on successive nights.

The battle pitted the Missouri State Guard, a pro-Southern force, against Union volunteer regiments. The Guard, under the direction of Missouri's secessionist governor, Claiborne Fox Jackson, consisted of 2,000 hastily assembled, poorly trained, and even some unarmed men. These troops faced 1,100 well-drilled, fully armed men led by Col. Franz Sigel. His men hoped to stop the Guard from reaching the southwest corner of the state and linking up with other Confederate forces to create an army of more than 10,000 men. Sigel's troops camped at Carter Spring, now part of the historic site, while Jackson's troops camped about 18 miles north.

On July 5, 1861, the two forces encountered each other near Dry Fork, about nine miles northwest of Carthage. The running battle started with an hour-long artillery duel, with Jackson attempting to surround Sigel's troops, and then Sigel ordering a retreat. A skirmish at Dry Fork Creek left the heaviest casualties. Sigel retreated into Carthage, where Jackson launched another infantry attack. While the fighting continued, house to house, Sigel positioned his artillery on the bluffs above Carter Spring, the location of the historic site. He successfully contin-

Left: Visitors can walk on the bluff above Carter Spring from which Union artillery fired the final battle shots, covering their withdrawal. *Denise H. Vaughn* • Right: Both federal and state troops, in conflict with each other, bivouacked in this meadow by Carter Spring on successive nights, July 4 and 5, 1861. *Missouri State Parks*

ued his retreat under the cover of darkness.

The Battle of Carthage illustrates the problems of preserving a site that isn't a well-bounded battlefield. At Carthage the action was fierce, but it lasted less than a day—never more than an hour or so at any one point—and it swept down nine miles of country road leaving no permanent marks. In 1990, legislation established the historic site focused on Carter Spring in the city of Carthage in Jasper County where federal and pro-South state forces ended the day's hostilities and where both sides bivouacked.

But the battle was much bigger than the Battle of Carthage State Historic Site and amorphous as well, as is often the case in the chaos of combat. As a result, the presentation is multifaceted. Park officials have placed an interpretive display at the state-owned spring site, but visitors also will want to see a city-owned Civil War museum near the square and take a self-guided auto tour along Civil War Avenue, driving the nine miles north to other scenes of action at Spring River, Buck Branch, and Dry Fork. Dry Fork, in particular, survives almost unaltered, its farm fields and creek probably looking much as they did on the day of the battle.

The battle at Carthage was small and not terribly significant. However, only at Carthage did a sitting governor, Gov. Claiborne Fox Jackson, personally and successfully lead state troops against a US army. It was also a turning point for the cause of the South in Missouri. It raised Southern hopes, and the Missouri State Guard gained momentum that carried it to Lexington, the high water mark of the Confederacy in Missouri. Carthage made it clear Union occupation of Missouri would be contested ferociously. ✴

Battle of Island Mound State Historic Site

4837 NW County Rd, Butler

This actor appeared in a film produced by Missouri State Parks about the battle. *Missouri State Parks*

AT MISSOURI'S WESTERN EDGE, the hills that seem to roll in from Kansas don't amount to much, but a small hill commands a big view. It is this landscape where African Americans fighting in the Civil War earned their place in Missouri—and national—history. The boundary between Kansas and Missouri runs through this country, and while only a line on a map, it was an important line, a significant part of the great national debate—a free soil territory on one side, a slave-holding state on the other. The 1820 Missouri Compromise and the 1854 Kansas-Nebraska Act that nullified it engendered a bloody, vicious conflict along this border between Free-Soilers in Kansas and pro-slavery adherents in Missouri, with nothing separating them but a line on the map. By the time the first shot at Fort Sumter was fired in 1861, a local civil war had already raged along the border for nearly a decade.

About nine miles east of this border in Missouri lay the Toothman farmstead, the site where on October 27, 1862, 240 blue-clad, black Union soldiers, the First Kansas Colored Volunteer Infantry, encamped and dubbed the camp Fort Africa. They had been sent to clear out a nest of pro-Southern guerrillas who occupied the ground between a channel of the Marais des Cygnes river and one of its wandering sloughs as a place of refuge and rest and for storage of supplies and loot. And so they did.

The Kansans were outnumbered about two-to-one by some four hundred mounted rebel guerrillas. On the flank of the river mounds, still a mile short of Fort Africa and no cover in sight, the beleaguered African American soldiers formed up and got off one volley of musket fire after another— as the rebel cavalry crashed into and over them—until the horsemen withdrew.

It wasn't much of a battle, but it was the first time in the Civil War that former slaves had taken up arms and performed admirably as soldiers on the battlefield. In fact, enlisting free black men and ex-slaves as Union soldiers had been debated since the Civil War began. Acting against President Abraham Lincoln's wishes and Secretary of War Edwin Stanton's orders, Kansas Senator Jim Lane, a radical instigator of many ugly border incidents, assembled two regiments of African Americans in 1862 as Kansas units. It was one of these regiments, not yet part of the federal army, at the Battle of Island Mound.

In 2008, the state bought forty acres, the site of Fort Africa, in time to prepare it for dedication on the 2012 sesquicentennial of the battle. The site to-day features a short trail—aptly named the Courage Trail—that leads out onto restored prairie where there is a view of the mounds on which the fighting took place on a farm adjacent to the site. Farther beyond, but out of sight behind the hills is the river bottomland.

Today, the countryside is still very open, but the prairie grasses have been mostly replaced by pastures and fields, and there are more trees on the high ground and fewer on the bottoms. A number of wayside markers with photos and maps explaining the battle are located along the trail.

The men of the First Kansas are commemorated in a bronze plaque, and visitors are accommodated with parking, a rest room, and a small pavilion for picnicking. A short stretch of rail fence calls to mind Fort Africa but mainly serves as a reminder that a rail fence was at least half air and didn't provide much protection from bullets. *

40 acres
Bates County

Trail
• Courage Trail (0.6 mi)

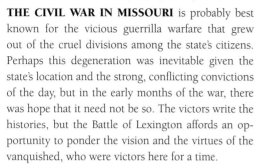

Battle of Lexington State Historic Site

1101 Delaware St, Lexington

THE CIVIL WAR IN MISSOURI is probably best known for the vicious guerrilla warfare that grew out of the cruel divisions among the state's citizens. Perhaps this degeneration was inevitable given the state's location and the strong, conflicting convictions of the day, but in the early months of the war, there was hope that it need not be so. The victors write the histories, but the Battle of Lexington affords an opportunity to ponder the vision and the virtues of the vanquished, who were victors here for a time.

An often overlooked factor of the Civil War in Missouri was the Missouri State Guard. This organization, never numbering more than 22,000 men at any one time, was surrounded on three sides by Northern states and defended the Southern cause west of the Mississippi for the better part of a year. The Missouri State Guard was the only border state army to make so bold a campaign and with little assistance from the official Confederate States Army.

The leader of the Missouri State Guard was probably the most popular man in Missouri. Sterling Price was a Virginia-born tobacco planter who had served Missouri as legislator and governor and his nation as congressman and brigadier general of Missouri volunteers in the Mexican War.

Price's rough and ready Missourians won for the South two of its most important victories west of the Mississippi. After they disbanded in 1862, Missouri State Guard veterans made up the core of some of the most highly regarded and decorated units in the regular Confederate States Army.

Perhaps the finest hour of the State Guard was its victory in September 1861 over the federal garrison at Lexington, on the Missouri River. It marked the high tide of hopes for uniting the state behind the pro-South government that Missourians had elected in 1860 and for driving the Union from the state.

In 1861 Lexington was a prosperous trading center for area tobacco and hemp plantations. Recognizing Lexington's importance, federal troops had occupied the town since July. Not far from the Union defenses was the stately home of one of Lafayette County's leading families, that of William Oliver Anderson. Married to a cousin of Sterling Price, Anderson refused to take an oath of loyalty to the federal government and was arrested and imprisoned.

Price arrived within sight of Lexington on September 12. After sharp skirmishes on the outskirts of town, Price waited for his supply wagons to catch up and then laid siege to the fortified garrison.

The Anderson house, which lay outside the Union

William Oliver Anderson's house was used as a field hospital during the battle. You can still see bullet holes in the house's walls and the outlines of Union defensive trenches here. *Missouri State Parks*

entrenchments, was being used by the federals as a hospital. Normally, both sides would have respected the neutrality of such a site, but the Anderson house was in too strategic a location to remain unmolested. As a result, it was attacked repeatedly by both sides.

Eventually, the Union troops succumbed to their opponents, who sheltered behind wet hemp bales as they pressed forward. They surrendered to Price. The battle was one of the last Civil War engagements to honor old-style warfare civilities. Price allowed federal officers to keep their swords and treated the opposing leader as a guest. The defeated enlisted men were praised for their bravery and paroled after being told to go home to Illinois and mind their own business.

The Tilton Davis family bought the Anderson house in 1865 and lived there for the next fifty years; you can see their furniture in some rooms today.

Lexington is brimming with history, beautiful Missouri valley scenery, and elegant architecture. It still evokes an antebellum Missouri river town. *

The battle is nicknamed the Battle of the Hemp Bales. Price's troops created novel, movable breastworks of hemp bales, soaked with water, to block bullets as they safely advanced.

**95 acres
Lafayette County**

Trail
- Battlefield Trail (0.3 mi)

Battle of Pilot Knob
State Historic Site

118 Maple St, Pilot Knob

ONE OF THE BLOODIEST BATTLES in Missouri took place at the Battle of Pilot Knob State Historic Site on September 27, 1864. Your tour here should begin in the visitor center, equipped with an audiovisual program telling the story of the battle that marked the beginning of the end for Confederate forces under Maj. Gen. Sterling Price. He made the fateful decision to attempt a frontal assault on Fort Davidson rather than leave this enemy fort on his flank, during his march toward St. Louis. But Union Brig. Gen. Thomas Ewing Jr.'s troops hung on during the day and then sneaked away during the night, blowing up the coveted powder magazine before they fled. You can see a fiber-optic battle map as well as other exhibits and artifacts, including a Confederate six-pounder cannon that had been dragged to the top of Shepherd Mountain only to be hit before it could be fired.

The approach to the fort is over a pleasant walking path. From the path toward the fort, the strategic nature of the narrow notch in the mountains becomes apparent. The mass of Shepherd Mountain looms ahead, blocking the horizon, while the jagged-toothed summit of Pilot Knob rears up behind. *

**77 acres
Iron County**

Trail
- Brogan's Trail (0.5 mi)

Historic Structure
- Earthwork fort

Top: Confederate reenactors replicate the doomed assault, stalling out in the dry moat surrounding the fort, just as soldiers did in 1864. Bottom: Fort Davidson was originally equipped with siege guns similar to this pair now displayed near the fort. *Both Ben Nickelson*

The spring was once known as Brice Spring. During the Civil War, Peter Bennett Jr. built a three-story mill with a timber dam and millrace.

3,339 acres
Dallas and Laclede Counties

Trails
- Bridge Trail (0.7 mi)
- Natural Tunnel Trail (7.5 mi)
- Oak Hickory Trail (0.3 mi)
- Savanna Ridge Trail (2.5 mi)
- Spring Trail (0.6 mi)
- Whistle Trail (1 mi)

Historic Structures
- CCC bridge, dam, cabins, store, post office, shelter houses, hatchery, roads, trails, and more

Bennett Spring State Park

26250 Rt 64A, Lebanon

FIGURES GARBED IN WADERS stroke the waters of Bennett Spring lovingly with their lines and, with rods extended, twitch the tips from time to time—homage to the sacred trout. To get to Bennett Spring, approaching from Highway 64 west of Lebanon, you wind down an entrance road past several private cottages and a tackle shop, then emerge from the upland into the hill-cradled valley.

On your right, you pass a sandstone-buttressed nature center, and the road curves over the stream on a graceful bridge of concrete and native stone, a now historic structure built in 1934 by the Civilian Conservation Corps (CCC). Upstream to your left is a low dam, successor to earlier milldams.

Over the bridge, you enter the village-like heart of the park. The lodge, containing a restaurant and meeting room, is another architectural gem from CCC days, its decorative chandeliers featuring a trout motif. In the park store, the concessionaire sells tackle and supplies to visitors and rents cabins and canoes for use on the nearby Niangua River; there is also a classroom for fishing instruction.

This was once the territory of the Osage Indians and earlier native peoples, whose legends suggest a special reverence for the spring, but they had already ceded their lands in Missouri when an early settler built a small gristmill on the spring branch.

The Natural Tunnel and Savanna Ridge Trails, totaling some ten miles with several loops, provide access to Spring Hollow and its woodlands seasonally abloom with wildflowers. Part of the trail goes through a twisting valley with steep cliffs, which are remainders of a collapsed cave system; the natural tunnel carved through the dolomite strata by the stream over geologic ages is in fact a cave, one that has been cut off by erosion of deeper valleys at each end.

Anglers and their families predominate among the almost 800,000 visitors at Bennett annually, but many others come to relax in the lodge, cabins, and campgrounds, to float the Niangua River, or to hike the trails through the scenic woodlands, awash in dogwood blooms each April. Everyone who comes, though, senses that the park is here because of the spring. And so are the trout. ✳

Top: The great spring at Bennett has always lured fishermen and women. It is the largest spring in any state park and gushes 100 million gallons a day. Its water holds steady at fifty-seven degrees Fahrenheit. *Missouri State Parks* • Middle: This 300-foot-long natural tunnel was created by the partial collapse of an ancient cave. *Diane Tucker* Bottom: Ten miles of loop trails take hikers through Spring Hollow woodlands ablaze with fall colors to a natural tunnel. *Scott Myers*

Thomas Hart Benton Home and Studio State Historic Site

3616 Belleview Ave, Kansas City

Tom and Rita Benton's two-and-a-half story, frame-and-stone house in Kansas City was comfortable and spacious. It sits amid towering trees and attractive shrubs and plants. *Ben Nickelson*

IN THE DEEP WINTER OF 1936-37, the cold weather was heated by a controversy that played loudly across the pages of the nation's newspapers. A war of words was waged over a painting, a mural in the House lounge of the state Capitol: "Whitewash the murals! They're vulgar! Nothing but honky-tonk, hillbillies, and robbers. We're more than a 'coon dog state!"

This mural, officially titled *A Social History of the State of Missouri*, was a spacious work in a distinguished place by a Missourian of eminent background. It was painted by Thomas Hart Benton, namesake great grandnephew of Missouri's first US senator.

By the mid-1930s, Tom Benton was no stranger to controversy, and he responded with vigor to his critics. He painted real folks along with some of the state's most characteristic folk legends. He captured for all time much of the pungent flavor of the state's history. Today, the Benton mural in the state Capitol is one of the most treasured artworks in the state; it inspires thousands of visitors every year. After seeing the mural, you will surely want to visit the home and studio of the artist who produced it and who came to be recognized as a preeminent representative of the Regionalist tradition in American art.

Moving to Kansas City was a sort of homecoming for Benton. Born in Neosho in 1889, Benton left home in his teens to pursue an art career; he lived for varying periods in Chicago, Paris, and New York. In the course of his travels, Benton became a recognized painter, though from almost the beginning a combative and controversial one. Benton gradually became disillusioned with much of the artistic establishment and East Coast life and came home to Missouri.

If Benton had produced no other work than the Capitol mural, he would still deserve a place in Missouri and American art history, but he produced thousands of illustrations, paintings, sketches, and other murals. Missourians love Benton best for his true rendering of working people and the land—he said he wanted to make "common art for the common man."

The home to which Tom and Rita Benton moved in 1939 and where they remained until their deaths in 1975 is located in midtown Kansas City. A portion of the carriage house was converted in the 1940s into Benton's art studio. Here we find today a linger-

ing presence of the artist. He was working the day he died, January 19, 1975, a heart attack having taken him as he was applying the finishing touches to another of his dynamic murals, *The Sources of Country Music*, for the Country Music Hall of Fame in Nashville.

Partly through the care and generosity of Benton's wife, who soon also passed away, and his friends, the artist's studio and home are almost perfectly preserved. They were purchased by the state in 1977 and opened to the public on April 15, 1983, the anniversary of his birth. In the studio, the furniture, paints, sketches, brushes, and even spectacles and a pipe lie about in perfectly natural clutter the way he left them.

In the home itself, almost all of the Bentons' personal possessions are also left in place. The most common and ordinary of family objects are as casually left as if Tom and Rita could walk in and offer us refreshment. In fact, entertaining friends from all over Missouri and well beyond was one of the great joys of household life for the Bentons. Their home had an atmosphere that encouraged visitors to return, and thanks to its preservation, it still does. *

In his capitol mural, Benton depicted a people and a state that he knew intimately and loved fiercely, but that he refused to idealize or romanticize.

**1 acre
Jackson County**

Big Lake State Park

204 Lake Shore Dr, Craig

THE MISSOURI RIVER HAS SHIFTED course across its floodplain over the years. After such a shift in course, the old channel often retained water and formed a marsh or lake. Where such an abandoned channel is the result of the river cutting off a U-shaped bend in its own course, the lake is called an oxbow lake. Big Lake is an oxbow lake with 615 acres of open water and nearby wildlife habitat.

As recently as a century or two ago, the floodplain of the Missouri River in northwest Missouri was a maze of shallow riverbeds, bottomland forests, wet prairies, marshes, and oxbow lakes teeming with fish, waterfowl, and large game animals. The floodplain was bordered on the east by high-piled mounds of savanna-covered loess. It was a lush and fertile landscape. Since having been channelized, the river no longer creates such a dynamic riparian corridor, except in vestiges still found in a few places along the western sections of a few northwestern counties, and in Big Lake State Park.

Most of northwest Missouri, including the silted-in former river channels, has been devoted to agricultural production, leaving relatively few areas to offer public opportunities for outdoor recreation. Big Lake does, and it has been a recreation magnet for many years. Much of its shoreline is dotted with weekend cabins and fishing camps. The primary attraction at Big Lake was the open water of the lake itself, and all developments—a campground, picnic areas, a swimming pool, a boat launch, vacation cabins, a restaurant, and a small motel—were oriented to viewing,

Big Lake is an oxbow lake and among the largest remaining natural oxbow lakes along the Missouri River. It is one of the largest natural lakes of any type in the state.

407 acres
Holt County

boating, and fishing opportunities in and around this shallow, tree-lined remnant of the Missouri River channel.

But the Missouri River over the years has had other ideas, occasionally flooding and depositing its silts in and around facilities, necessitating major cleanups and renovations. After the devastating flood of 2011 destroyed virtually all the facilities, the park remained closed for three years. It reopened with a campground, boat launch, and picnic area, and it now boasts eight camper cabins on wheels that can be moved to high ground when the river floods. The park is now less prone to flood damage in the future.

As the Missouri River does what it will, the oxbow lakes, sloughs, and other wetlands continue to attract millions of migratory waterfowl and provide a haven for resident birds and animals. Big Lake has the largest natural Missouri River floodplain marsh in our parks. It is a refuge for the unusual yellow-headed blackbird, and there always seem to be shorebirds or waterfowl on the lake. Snow geese make a thunderous display during their migration in the spring and fall, and bald eagles soar over the park.

Water is pumped into the lake to keep it deep enough for fishing and boating. A new portion of the park known as Scout Island is a fine place to walk to see floodplain plants and birds or to drop a line for Missouri River catfish.

So, in the midst of heavily farmed northwest Missouri, there is an oasis of recreation, natural landscape, and wildlife. Come in the summer for a lazy camp-out and fishing trip or during spring or fall migration time—or even in winter—to watch the eagles. Big Lake is a special retreat in the magnificent Missouri valley. ✴

Left: A great blue heron rises majestically from the marsh. In the spring and fall, hundreds of migratory waterfowl also visit Big Lake. *Missouri State Parks* • Right: Big Lake provides opportunities for fishing and bird-watching in northwest Missourian. *Stephanie Sidoti*

Big Oak Tree State Park

13640 S Rt 102, East Prairie

PICKING OUT THE BOUNDARIES of Big Oak Tree State Park is easy as you drive south on Route 102 from East Prairie, across the billiard-table-flat farmlands of Mississippi County. The one-thousand-acre preserve stands out as an oasis of tall trees surrounded by miles of cropland, a living time capsule for an environment that once stretched across the entire Bootheel of southeastern Missouri.

Big Oak Tree is a monument both to the original forested wilderness of "swampeast" Missouri and to the dedication of citizens who wished to ensure that at least a small fragment of that vast wilderness would be forever protected from logging and agricultural development. The park also stands as testimony to the difficulty of trying to protect a dynamic ecosystem no longer connected to many of the flooding processes that shaped it over time.

Your first impression is of the height of the forest and the size of the trees. The canopy rises to 120 feet, with some of the park's giants grabbing another twenty feet of sky. For a time in the 1960s, this small park in Missouri's Mississippi Lowlands was home to nine reigning national champions on the American Forestry Association's roster of big trees; that is, nine trees were the largest recorded representatives of their species anywhere in the nation. Today, Big Oak Tree Park is still home to one national champion, a pumpkin ash, and three state champion trees, overcup oak, sweetgum, and persimmon.

The park has the only bottomland hardwood forest to survive essentially uncut out of the 2.5 million acres in Missouri of the great Mississippi floodplain forest that once stretched from southeastern Missouri to the Gulf of Mexico.

Bird-watchers visit to record some of the park's more than 150 known species, several rare in Missouri. The bright yellow plumage of the hooded warbler makes it easier to spot than some other warblers, such as the rare and secretive Swainson's. A loud "AAH-aah" from the fish crow might pierce the woods, and high overhead, you might see the Mississippi kite.

With ongoing restoration of a more natural flood cycle, Big Oak Tree State Park will endure and remain a remarkable and unique testament to the presettlement biological richness of the swamp-forest ecosystem where those big oaks were born. *

The great bur oak that inspired the park lived here for 396 years. Once scheduled to be cut down as a curiosity for the 1904 World's Fair, the tree survived another half-century before succumbing in 1952 to lightning strikes and tree rot.

1,029 acres
Mississippi County

Trails
- Boardwalk Trail (0.7 mi)
- Bottomland Trail (1.5 mi)
- Cypress Trail (.8 mi)

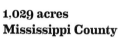

Top: A boardwalk leads visitors into the swamp. *Scott Myers* • Middle: After the 2011 flood degraded the lake berm, it began reverting to a more natural swamp pond, and cypresses began recovering. *Ron Colatskie* • Bottom: Bald cypress dominated the swamps of what used to be called "swampeast" Missouri before it was drained for farming. *Ken McCarty*

Big Sugar Creek State Park

7126 Big Sugar Creek Rd, Pineville

This park is one of the only places in Missouri where the Ozark Chinquapin survives and may provide seeds for reestablishment of the species.

2,083 acres McDonald County

Trail
- Ozark Chinquapin Trail (3.25 mi)

Historic Structures
- Rock outbuilding for Shady Grove School
- House and granary foundations from the hamlet of Cyclone

LIKE THE CRYSTALS OF A GEODE within an ordinary rock, Big Sugar Creek is a treasure amid far southwest Missouri's remote hills. It boasts a diverse array of living communities and limestone glades that harbor rare, endangered, and regionally restricted plants and animals. The rugged hills of McDonald County have also given rise to legends, tall tales, and a fascinating history, with considerable uncertainty as to which is which.

There are stories of Pine Wars, with battles fought over rights to valuable pine timber, and a real war, when Northern and Southern armies marched through the county and no one could be safely neutral. The courthouse was burned by bushwhackers in 1863, and in 1939, many scenes in the famous movie *Jessie James* were filmed nearby because Hollywood executives thought Pineville and the Big Sugar country looked more like 1870s Clay County than Clay County did. A place on the river known as Penitentiary Bend is claimed by some as the site where a sheriff's posse rounded up a band of outlaws; others maintain as stoutly that miserable prisoners from a Civil War skirmish were once confined there.

The park includes two-and-a-half miles of riverfront, a fine setting for river play and exploration, but unlike most rivers in the Missouri Ozarks that drain north, east, and south to the Missouri, Mississippi, and White Rivers, Big Sugar Creek drains southwest into the Elk River and then on to the great Arkansas

River drainage, a distinct and powerful landscape. As a result, this clear-water, bedrock stream harbors some aquatic species unique to this area of the state, including the redspot chub, bluntface shiner, cardinal shiner, Neosho midget crayfish, and mucket mussel. The range of steep hills and rocky hollows that cradle the Big Sugar valley provide habitat for a rich array of species and communities, including the rare Ozark Chinquapin tree. A variety of unusual animals also find refuge within the Big Sugar Hills, including the gray bat, Oklahoma salamander, and pine warbler.

The topography that makes this area a joy to visit today also slowed early settlement. The first land patents were taken out in the 1830s, and by 1860 there was a low dam across Big Sugar providing power for a gristmill. A small store provided goods, but this hamlet didn't get its formal name, Cyclone, until 1883.

In 2016 a total of 1,168 acres of the park was designated the Elk River Hills Wild Area, the first wild area designated in the state since 1995. A key feature of the wild area is the three-mile Ozark Chinquapin Trail. The trail gives you a chance to experience this rough terrain as Native Americans and early explorers may have, traversing ancient ridges and valleys through which spring water and rainwater flow in myriad deep hollows to Big Sugar Creek. You might chance upon a whitetail buck along the trail or see a roadrunner, a Southwestern species.

Big Sugar is a landscape of rugged beauty and much remaining mystery. It reminds us of our state's links to the great Southwest, and it deserves a visit from Missourians curious about the fascinating nooks and crannies of their wonderful state. ∗

Left: The roadrunner and other species are more commonly seen in the south and west. *El Brujo* • Big Sugar Creek journeys southwest into the Arkansas River drainage area from the wild Elk River hills. Oaks and scattered shortleaf pine are common here. *Susan Flader.*

Bollinger Mill Historic Site

113 Bollinger Mill Rd, Burfordville

The original buhrstones used in the mill, which were imported from France, have been restored and are still on display for visitors to see.

44 acres
Cape Girardeau County

THE BURFORDVILLE BRIDGE spans the Whitewater River just upstream from Bollinger Mill in an area that was a wilderness in the 1790s when George Bollinger arrived.

Bollinger received a Spanish land grant on condition that the land be developed and settled. He built the first mill and dam of logs at the turn of the nineteenth century, and he also brought twenty German and Swiss families from his home state of North Carolina to the settlement along with German-speaking slaves of their households. Bollinger would go on to serve as an officer in the War of 1812 and a statesman.

After Bollinger died in 1842, his family operated the mill until September 1861, when it was razed by Union troops in retaliation for an attack carried out by one of Bollinger's confederate grandsons.

In 1865, Solomon R. Burford rebuilt the mill, the four-story structure full of milling machines that visitors enjoy touring today. The mill ceased commercial operation around 1948, but its machinery has been painstakingly restored for demonstrations.

Today, Bollinger Mill and Burfordville Covered Bridge provide the visitor with a step back in time to experience genuine grist milling, a stroll through the oldest covered bridge in Missouri, and a peaceful rest along a tree-lined stream. *

Top: Surviving nineteenth-century mills and covered bridges are rare, and even rarer side by side. *Jim Diaz* • Above: Visitors can inspect this Leffel turbine, like the one submerged in the river that ran the mill and still turns the stones today to grind cornmeal. *Denise H. Vaughn*

Nathan and Olive Boone Homestead State Historic Site

7850 N Hwy V, Ash Grove

At the time of Nathan's death in 1856, local residents referred to the Boone home as Boone mansion.

400 acres
Greene County

Trails
• Homestead Interpretive Trail (0.5 mi)
• Spring Box Trail (1 mi)
• Prairie View Trail (2.4 mi)

COL. NATHAN BOONE, SOLDIER, surveyor, explorer, and son of the famous pioneer, was starting over again at the age of fifty-seven when he had to sell his handsome stone house and land in St. Charles County, possibly to get out of debt, and move his family to a hand-hewn dogtrot log cabin at Ash Grove northwest of Springfield.

The site of the new Boone farm was in a shallow swale formed by a tributary of Clear Creek, which runs west to the Sac River a mile and a half away. The landscape, now partially restored to native prairie flora with limestone glades that harbor thriving populations of the endangered Missouri bladderpod plant, probably looks today much as it did when Nathan first saw it. Patches of trees stand along the creek, and small woodlands mark the family burial plot and several springs. The house here was far less grand than the one he'd left in St. Charles County.

Nathan was able to enjoy his new home on the prairie only on sporadic furloughs between his army assignments. Olive stayed here and cared for her aged mother (who lived to 104), her younger daughters, several orphaned grandchildren, and other relatives while managing the farm and five to fifteen slaves during Nathan's long absences. The farm had hogs, cows, sheep, horses, oxen, and several hundred acres of land growing corn, oats, potatoes, and wheat.

In 1848, Nathan took sick leave and returned to Ash Grove. He never again saw active duty and resigned his commission at age seventy-two in 1853. He rode over his farm checking on crops and livestock when he was able and enjoyed sitting on the veranda telling stories of his adventures. When he died in 1856, he was buried a few hundred yards north of the house. Two years later, Olive died; she had once been his sixteen-year-old bride. There they still lie, amid some of their grandchildren.

The luck of Boones with land had never run smoothly, and even this last homestead was entangled in a court fight among Nathan and Olive's children and then left the Boone family entirely in 1897, when it was sold to cover a Boone grandchild's debt. Perhaps fate finally smiled on August 15, 1991, when the Missouri Department of Natural Resources took title to 370 acres of original Boone land. There will now be a Boone homestead on the map in perpetuity, as if the grateful citizens of their adopted state are holding in trust for this illustrious pioneer family the land that eluded them in their own lifetimes. *

Top: Black-eyed Susan and wild bergamot brighten the homestead. *Scott Myers* • Middle: An heirloom garden reminds visitors that settlers grew most of their food. • Bottom: Olive Boone's loom would have been in the breezeway or the living room of the cabin. The loom here is from another Boone family. *Both Bonnie Roggensees*

Boone's Lick State Historic Site

Rt 187, Boonesboro

NATHAN AND DANIEL MORGAN BOONE began manufacturing salt at a Missouri valley site in what is now southwestern Howard County in 1805. The Boone brothers later left the salt business, but their enterprise gave these salt springs and this interior region of Missouri a new name. The trail the Boones blazed from St. Charles to the salt springs, known as the Boone's Lick Trail, was followed by thousands of pioneers who bypassed eastern Missouri to settle the rich farmlands of the Missouri Valley.

Salt springs, or salines, were desirable in a frontier society and common in this part of the state, though few were as large or as well-known as Boone's Lick. Lewis and Clark recorded "a large lick and salt spring of great strength" about four miles southeast of "a cliff called the Arrow Rock" on their trip up the Missouri in 1804.

In an interview more than four decades later in 1851, Nathan Boone said they initially had six to eight men using forty kettles and one furnace to boil the brine water. They produced twenty-five to thirty bushels of salt a day and boated them to settlements downriver where salt sold readily for two-and-a-half dollars per bushel. As the business grew, they added furnaces and kept fifteen to twenty men employed, making 130 bushels a day. Each worker was paid about fifteen dollars a month.

The Daughters of the American Revolution marked the site of Boone's Lick in the early twentieth century, but it remained relatively unknown. Then in

Left: A short trail leads to the springs where the Boone brothers made salt. When the weather is right, you can smell sulfurous vapors. *Sarah Hackman* • Right: A wooden well casing has survived for more than a century, preserved by the saline water. *Missouri State Parks*

1960, Mr. and Mrs. J. R. Clinkscales of Boonville and Horace Munday donated to the State Park Board two small tracts that contained what remained of the salt lick. At first, the site required a visitor to exercise his or her imagination.

Over the following decades, however, there were several important discoveries. In 1986 a brief ten-day archaeological investigation led by Robert T. Bray found not one furnace as in 1961, or two as reported by Nathan Boone, or four as reported by Jesse Morrison, but six rock-lined furnaces. Four years later, another investigation would raise that number to ten. Moreover, the remains of several well casings, two log cabins, and a brine-elevating delivery system were still there underground, perfectly preserved in the waterlogged, briny earth.

Most remarkable of all was a ten-foot-long octagonal shaft superbly hand-hewn from a log. It was the drive shaft for a tread wheel designed to dip brine from the spring and elevate it to a system of wooden flumes to supply the various furnaces. The 960-pound drive shaft required twelve people to carry it up the hill to be transported.

The park contains about fifty acres set among rolling fields and wooded hills. A kiosk explains how salt was made. A narrow, winding trail among wooded hills leads down into the spring valley. An original cast-iron salt kettle and remnants of two well casings are still visible on site, and the drive shaft can be seen in the visitor center across the river at Arrow Rock State Historic Site. Boone's Lick today is off the beaten track and so peaceful that you can scarcely imagine it as the scene of a noisy, smoky frontier industry. *

Some of the grasses found around this and other similar licks in the area, such as salt meadow grass, might seem more at home along the seashore.

51 acres
Howard County

Trail
- Boone's Lick Interpretive Trail (0.2 mi)

Bothwell Lodge
State Historic Site

19349 Bothwell State Park Rd, Sedalia

John Homer Bothwell's Stonyridge estate, located north of Sedalia, was added to the state park system in 1974. The structure has been intriguing guests since the turn of the twentieth century. *Oliver Schuchard*

THE STONE CASTLE standing prominently on a bluff just a few miles north of Sedalia along Highway 65 and the surrounding 180 acres were dedicated in 1979 as Bothwell State Park, later changed to Bothwell Lodge State Historic Site. Additional acreage has since been added. John Homer Bothwell, a Pettis County attorney and businessman, moved to Missouri in 1871 and married the daughter of a prominent Sedalia family, Hattie Ellen Jaynes. Hattie died only a few years later after contracting an unknown illness, and Bothwell never remarried. He was active in local politics and served Pettis County in the Missouri General Assembly for four terms. He also ran unsuccessfully for governor in 1904, and helped make Sedalia the State Fair's permanent home.

After purchasing the bluff-top property in 1896, Bothwell began construction of the home he called Stonyridge Farm. He used native rock from the estate grounds, and the house grew in a rambling fashion. Four independent sections are tied together. In a combination storage area and workroom below the library, a wooden box covers an opening to a shaft that drops directly into a cave below the house. The shaft links the cave to a winding stairwell in the tower, which has doors and windows that can be opened to create a draft that pulls naturally cooled air up into the house.

As a bachelor of means, Bothwell enjoyed both traveling afar and entertaining guests. His lodge reflected all of this in its informal atmosphere and eclectic furnishings, from Mission style to wicker, with souvenirs from his travels and the odd stuffed and mounted animal. Bothwell appreciated the natural world, and he grieved that much of the timber atop the ridge had been cut just before he bought the property. He spent years restoring the native vegetation around his estate, and he built a half-mile trail along the wooded slope surrounding the lodge, with stone steps in steep spots, benches for resting, and a small picnic shelter.

Bothwell prospered into his old age, continuing to provide easy-going hospitality until his death in 1929, and even after. His will provided that the estate should continue to serve as a recreational retreat for his friends and ultimately for the people of Missouri.

A trip to this site properly begins with a visit to the lodge, which could be described as an overgrown English cottage. It has three levels and thirty rooms; twenty are visible on tour. If Hattie Bothwell had lived, she might have brought a more delicate touch to the decor, but the furnishings are of good quality and comfortable. A favorite room is the library; when you go inside, it's easy to imagine the widely read and curious Bothwell amidst the fine woodwork, enjoying his extensive collection of handsomely housed books, including many early and limited editions from the 1870s and 1880s, as well as the lovely view of the valley below his estate. The cozy fireplace must have made this a favorite retreat in the wintertime, too.

Bothwell's Stonyridge Trail has been refurbished and still offers a pleasant walk. Many of the trees along this forested slope are sugar maples, so fall walks can be especially beautiful among the orange and golden leaves. In 2006, the site opened a longer and more challenging three-mile route, the Radiant Trail, named after a favorite poem of John Bothwell. He believed above all in enjoying nature's radiance and bequeathed his home and grounds to the state so future generations of Missourians could also enjoy them. ✳

247 acres
Pettis County

Trails
- Radiant Trail (3.2 mi)
- Stonyridge Trail (0.5 mi)

Bryant Creek State Park

Hwy 5, south of Ava

The park's steep hills and deep hollows include scenic oak and pine forests that feature large old trees, mossy fern-draped sandstone outcrops and sheer dolomite bluffs.

2,917 acres
Douglas County

THE MOST PRIMITIVE and pristine of four new state parks in the Ozarks is Bryant Creek.

The park consists of 2,917 acres of rugged hills, forested in impressively large oaks and shortleaf pines. Some of the trees may be up to three hundred years old, with the largest on hillsides that have been uncut.

Three deep hollows, green with mosses, ferns, and lichen, lead down through sandstone outcrops to the park's namesake.

Bryant Creek is a clear Ozark stream with a reputation for fine smallmouth bass fishing. It is lined with gray dolomite bluffs as it borders the park on the north for some two miles.

Much of the creek is shallow, with scattered deep holes. Riffles run by the occasional gravel bar, and side chutes veer off from the main channel under a canopy of sun-dappled light.

The ridgetop has a beautiful pine forest with views up and down the valley of Bryant Creek. The river bottoms include dense stands of cane; during one visit, park staffers flushed two black bears out of a canebrake.

The current management plan calls for rehabilitation of old farm fields into native grasses and flowers, preservation of the glades and mature forests and regeneration of woodlands that have been cut.

Once the park opens, visitors will be able to ex-

Bryant Creek winds through the park and has a reputation for fine smallmouth bass fishing. Gray dolomite bluffs line much of the creek, and sometimes boulders tumble right in. *Both Tom Uhlenbrock*

plore the trails to get a true backcountry wilderness experience. People who float the creek can already set up camp on a gravel bar and fish for their supper.

The only sounds greeting a visitor will be the rippling of the water, the chattering-sound of the pileated woodpeckers and the haunting calls of the barred owls. Dark nights bring out a full canvas of stars. *

Castlewood State Park

1401 Kiefer Creek Rd, Ballwin

The park contributes greatly to the goal of establishing a greenbelt along more than 100 miles of the lower Meramec River, with public and private recreation facilities and interconnecting trail systems.

**1,818 acres
St. Louis County**

Trails

- Al Foster Trail (4.7 mi)
- Castlewood Loop (2.75 mi)
- Cedar Bluff Loop (2.25 mi)
- Chubb Trail (6.5 mi)
- Grotpeter Trail (3.75 mi)
- Lone Wolf Trail (1.5 mi)
- River Scene Trail (3.25 mi)
- Stinging Nettle Trail (2.5 mi)

ST. LOUISANS FLOCKED by the thousands to the Castlewood area from 1915 to about 1940 for weekends of canoeing, swimming, dancing, partying, and some gambling. After World War II, many of the hotels and clubhouses declined, and the natural beauty and recreational value of the lower Meramec River went unappreciated as the area became a kind of industrial dumping ground.

Today much of the dormant potential of the river has been rediscovered. In 1975 Gov. Christopher Bond announced a plan to coordinate the recovery of more than a hundred miles of the lower Meramec River. The centerpiece of this effort was and is Castlewood State Park, which offers more than thirty miles of hiking and biking trails, eleven of which are open to horseback riders.

A hike along the River Scene Trail leads one atop the white cherty limestone bluffs where a truly majestic view awaits. Look south across the river's floodplain into the wooded alcoves of Tyson Valley, upstream as the bluffs arc to the southwest or downstream as far as Fenton.

Across the river some 250 feet below—now grown up in willows—is the old Lincoln Beach, a sandy byproduct of the Union Sand and Gravel Company's gravel-mining activity in the river upstream.

On the south side of the river near the old community site of Morschels is a stand of native bottomland forest. Most such stands were long ago cleared away for agriculture or industry, but here at Castlewood, the visitor can still experience the feel of a mature floodplain forest with its silver maple, box elder, black willow, white ash, sycamore, slippery elm, and hackberry. By contrast, as you enter the park via Ries Road from the north, a beautiful drive along Kiefer Creek's canyon-like descent, you pass through the more typical upland forest of the eastern Ozark Border, dominated by white oak, northern red oak, and shagbark hickory. If it is spring, the floral displays of the redbud and dogwood will highlight your drive.

The Kiefer Creek Watershed Restoration Project has been a success story, and today it's inviting for play on a hot summer day. The legacy of grand weekend recreation that once defined Castlewood State Park is still alive and well here, and the park has also become a testament to environmental stewardship. *

Top: Thirty miles of trails invite all kinds of recreation. Visitors can hike, bike, and play in the water along the Meramec River. *Missouri State Parks* • Middle: Kiefer Creek is a magnet for children on a hot summer day. *Scott Myers* • Bottom: Bluff-top views at Castlewood are among the best in the park system. *Missouri State Parks*

Clark's Hill/Norton State Historic Site

Osage Hickory St, Osage City

CLARK'S HILL IS A TRIPLE-BONUS sort of place, interesting geologically, geographically, and historically. Plus, it provides one of the finest overlook views of the Missouri River valley that can be had.

Meriwether Lewis and William Clark camped here in 1804, and again on their return trip in 1806. On the morning of June 2, 1804, Clark left the riverbank camp and climbed the hill, which he estimated to have been one hundred feet high.

Today, the park provides an easy walk to the top of the high riverside bluff via a trail through the woods. The trail offsets the steepness of the climb by making a few switchbacks, trading length for slope. Along the way, visitors pass by five Native American burial mounds along the edge of the bluff.

The hill is densely wooded today, but in a few open, sunny clearings, wildflowers can be seen. In winter, eagles sometimes fish the rivers lying just below. Although the valley is always on view, the best look at the rivers themselves is in the wintertime, when the surrounding trees are bare.

Up and down both rivers, the dense bottomland forests are mostly gone now, and a patchwork of crops and plowed fields recedes into the distance. But the hill itself remains the same, as do its five burial mounds, there for a thousand years. ✳

Zebulon Pike led an exploration party by this hill and up the Osage River at nearly the same time as Lewis and Clark were returning down the Missouri River from the northwest in 1806. The two parties missed each other by a month.

13 acres
Cole County

Trail
- Osage Trail (0.5 mi)

Top: William Clark would have seen a much wider Missouri River than visitors see today. *Missouri State Parks* • Clark's Hill is above the present confluence of the Osage River on the left and the Missouri River, at the tip of the triangular patch of yellow grain in the distance where the two rivers come closest together. The hill now adjoins a peninsula that is the former Big (or Dodd's) Island. The thin white line is a road on the levee that separates the rivers. Most bottomland along the channelized Missouri River is now in row crops. *Jim Wark*

Confederate Memorial State Historic Site

211 W 1st St, Higginsville

The epitaph on the headstone of the last veteran at the home to be buried is itself a lesson in history, and none who see it leave unmindful of the Southern cause in Missouri or unmoved by the devotion of its followers. It reads simply: "John T. Graves, the last of Shelby's men, 1842-1950."

**135 acres
Lafayette County**

IN MISSOURI'S LITTLE DIXIE, not far from the Missouri River, the Confederate Memorial State Historic Site commemorates more than fifty thousand Missouri soldiers who fought for the Confederacy. It is a testimonial also to their wives and daughters, who bore the brunt of the war at home and who a generation or so later took the lead in establishing the home, grounds, and cemetery where so many of the veterans came to live out their last years and be buried.

In the 1880s, veterans who organized as the Ex-Confederate Association of Missouri came together to relive old times and to consider the plight of the less fortunate among them. They incorporated a Confederate Home Association to select a site and seek funding for a home for their destitute brethren. Practically every state that furnished organized troops for the Confederacy established homes for veterans, but Missouri was unique in building and furnishing its home solely through voluntary contributions. This is where the women entered the picture.

Seeking a way to aid the cause of the Confederate Home, Mrs. Abner Cassidy of St. Louis invited nearly one hundred women to the Southern Hotel in that city in January 1891 to organize the Daughters of the Confederacy and to promote a plan for selling tickets at ten cents apiece, each representing "a brick in the Confederate Home." The idea caught on and soon spread to other communities and then other states.

The home was dedicated in 1893 and six months later had 115 residents. The Daughters of the Confederacy subsequently built a hospital, a chapel, and several other buildings. At its height, the Confederate Home annually cared for more than 380 veterans and their families, and the property consisted of thirty buildings and a thriving dairy and farm. In 1925 the hospital board proposed development of a memorial park. About ninety acres were landscaped and thousands of trees and shrubs planted, again courtesy of the Daughters of the Confederacy with the help of local schoolchildren. Seven lakes were built and stocked with fish. A footbridge, gazebo, and bandstand were constructed, all at no expense to the state. The site was deeded over to the State Park Board in 1949.

The United Daughters of the Confederacy gave the cemetery to the State Park Board in 1952, to be managed in conjunction with the memorial park that had been accepted three years earlier. The chapel, threatened with demolition, was saved in 1978 by the Higginsville chapter of the Beta Sigma Phi sorority, who paid to move it back near its original site next to the cemetery on state park land.

Today, Confederate Memorial Park is administered as a beautiful historic site. The simple, one-room frame chapel, one of only two such Confederate memorial chapels still standing (the other is in Richmond, Virginia), has been restored and furnished, with exhibits in the basement about the history of the home. The lake area, ever popular for fishing and picnicking, has been restored to look as it did when built by the Daughters of the Confederacy. The fishing is still good, and the grounds are still peaceful. *

Left: The Confederate Memorial Chapel is one of only two such chapels in the country that still remain to honor the vanquished. *David Piet* • Right: The Missouri Daughters of the Confederacy commissioned this monument modeled on the Lion of Lucerne in Switzerland, dedicated to Swiss Guards massacred during the French Revolution. Mark Twain described the original as "the most mournful and moving piece of stone in the world." *Oliver Schuchard*

Edward "Ted" and Pat Jones–Confluence Point State Park

1000 Riverlands Way, West Alton

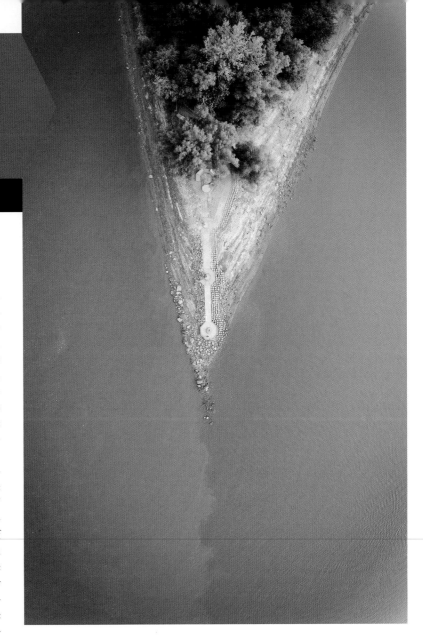

A drone view of the confluence shows the waters of America's two great rivers as they begin to mingle. The Mississippi is on the right, and the Missouri is on the left. The point is a rocky spit of land. *Paul Jackson*

THE FRENCH EXPLORER Father Pierre Francois-Xavier de Charlevoix captured the essence of the place in 1721: "I believe this is the finest confluence in the world. The two rivers are much the same breadth, each about half a league: but the Missouri is by far the most rapid, and seems to enter the Mississippi like a conqueror, through which it carries its white waters to the opposite shore without mixing them; afterwards, it gives its color to the Mississippi which it never loses again but carries quite down to the sea." Of course, Father Charlevoix is describing the two rivers themselves, not the surrounding land. The early explorers of this area didn't care much about the land at the confluence, preferring instead to conduct their explorations by canoe on the river highways.

Perhaps the first person to give serious consideration to the land around the confluence would have been Capt. Don Francesco Rui y Morales. In 1767 after France ceded Louisiana to Spain, the royal Spanish governor in New Orleans sent Rui and a crew of soldiers and laborers to build two forts, one on each side of the mouth of the Missouri River, to deny the British any opportunity to ascend that stream. In New Orleans this looked good on paper, but when Captain Rui arrived at the confluence, he found that the north bank at the mouth was under nine feet of water. What was obvious to the Europeans—and later, Americans—on the scene was that the considerable plain surrounding the confluence in every direction was one large wetland, nearly all of which went under water almost every year.

The park is named in honor of Edward "Ted" Jones and his wife Pat, who donated funds for the establishment of Katy Trail State Park.

The Edward "Ted" and Pat Jones–Confluence Point State Park was dedicated on Sunday, May 9, 2004, with a replica pirogue and Lewis and Clark expedition reenactors present for the event. This was most appropriate, as that great Voyage of Discovery began here at the confluence on May 14, 1804.

Park naturalists have undertaken significant restoration activities since the park's opening in 2004, and the land has begun to more closely resemble descriptions contained in historical accounts. With only a dozen feet of vertical relief and roughly ten different soil types, restoration means re-creation of diverse habitats ranging from sandbars and mudflats to bottomland forest, prairie, marsh, and shrub swamp. The ultimate goal for the park is the reestablishment of more natural floodplain function including native vegetation and natural wetlands, which will allow visitors to experience something of what early explorers saw when encountering the area.

On the actual rocky point where the two greatest rivers on the continent join together, you can walk out to the point and plant one foot in the Missouri and one in the Mississippi River. But you can also ponder the meeting of these waters and their roles in the exploration and development of the nation. If you are lucky, you may see pelicans wheeling and spiraling above the point, trumpeter swans migrating up or downriver, or a bald eagle standing sentinel in a nearby tree. State parks are often landmarks, and it would be difficult to imagine a single geographic point with more meaning than this place. ✳

The park has such low elevation that flooding can be expected for at least thirty consecutive days every ten years.

1,121 acres
St. Charles County

Trail

- Confluence Point Trail (.3 mi)

Crowder State Park

76 NW Rt 128, Trenton

NESTLED IN THE ROLLING HILLS of north-central Missouri, Crowder State Park memorializes Gen. Enoch Crowder, a native of the area, and offers a retreat of rugged slopes and stately forests in a region consisting generally of level farmland.

Crowder was born in 1859 and went to West Point. Early in his career in the 1880s, he participated in efforts to corral Geronimo and his Apache band. Later, he served as military governor of the Philippines and also as the first ambassador to Cuba. But he is best remembered as the "father of the Selective Service." As judge advocate general, Crowder drafted the Selective Service Act of 1917 and directed its implementation.

There is general consensus that the Selective Service System was a key factor in the United States' victorious role in World War I. The law that established the draft, an extension of the idea of the citizen soldier, inspired one waggish county clerk to versify about the local sheriff named Burke and himself, when he was "drafted" into helping to implement it: "Who was it built up this army, that set the whole world free?/Who inducted them into service? It was Crowder, and Burke, and me."

The leader of American forces in World War I and a fellow north Missourian, Gen. John J. Pershing commented following Crowder's death in 1932: "Professionally his exceptional record speaks for itself.... I had a high regard for him, both as a man and an officer." He is buried in Arlington Cemetery.

The park is located just a few miles from the Crowder homestead. The park's rich glacial soils nurture thick forests of sugar maple and stately white and red oaks. A campground sits on a hill above a lake, and one of the park system's fine group camps, Camp Grand River, sits upon a broad ridge above the Big Thompson tributary of the Grand, which borders a portion of the park. Like most streams in north Missouri, the Big Thompson was channelized in the 1920s, but the stretch in the park once again twists and bends around sandbars and gnarled driftwood snags. A bottomland forest of silver maple, cottonwood, river birch, sycamore, and green ash shade a valley floor where the rare ostrich fern grows. On well-shaded sandstone ledges, lady slipper orchids and maidenhair ferns cling to a delicate existence.

The park honors Crowder but its natural and recreational appeal draws 100,000 visitors a year. ✳

Top: The park has miles of interconnected hiking, biking, and horse trails. *Missouri State Parks* • Middle: A twenty-acre lake offers boating and fishing. *Anna Persell* • Bottom: The Big Thompson River once again meanders across the glacial till plain. *Don Schultehenrich*

The park has several mounds built by prehistoric native peoples, and it was still occupied by the Sac and Fox tribes when American settlers showed up.

1,912 acres
Grundy County

Trails

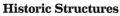

- Red Bud Trail (1.75 mi)
- River Forks Trail (2 mi)
- Tall Oaks Trail (3 mi)
- Thompson River Trail (8.6 mi)

Historic Structures
- CCC rock bridge and CCC rock wall

Cuivre River State Park

678 State Rt 147, Troy

CUIVRE RIVER BARELY TOUCHES the southwestern edge of the state park that bears its name in Lincoln County. But the juxtaposition is dramatic: a high cliff of Mississippian limestone known locally as Frenchman's Bluff drops off sharply to the river. From the vantage point of the park, one can take in a sweeping view.

Such striking topography may, at first, seem out of place north of the Missouri River. The rugged landscape, the rich woodlands, the limestone glades, the upland sinkhole ponds: all seem more representative of the Ozarks region south of the river. But Cuivre (pronounced quiver) River State Park is located at the southern end of a sixty-mile stretch of uplifted bedrock known as the Lincoln Hills. While continental glaciers scoured and buried the land north of the Missouri River with debris, the Lincoln Hills somehow escaped most of this.

American Indians arrived in the area as early as ten thousand years ago, and archaeologists have identified their villages, campsites, burial mounds, and ceremonial areas in and around the park. French explorers and settlers came next, hence the names for the bluff and the river: *cuivre* means copper in French, but some think the river was originally named in honor of Georges Cuvier, a noted French paleontologist and naturalist.

Cuivre River is one of three state parks initially acquired by the National Park Service as Recreation Demonstration Areas (RDAs) through the 1933 National Industrial Recovery Act. RDAs were supposed

....

Left: Many woodland wildflowers have responded vigorously to controlled burns and dot the savanna-like border of the Lincoln Glade area. *Bruce Schuette* • Right: The hot sun and the cool water beckon swimmers at the Lake Lincoln beach. *Missouri State Parks*

In 1978 a small natural area was designated to protect Pickerelweed Pond, a three-quarter-acre pond. By 1997 it had been expanded to the 1,872-acre Lincoln Hills Natural Area— the park's crown jewel.

**6,427 acres
Lincoln County**

Trails
- Big Sugar Creek Trail (3.75 mi)
- Blackhawk Point Trail (5.75 mi)
- Blazing Star Trail (2 mi)
- Cuivre River Trail (11.25 mi)
- Frenchman's Bluff (1.5 mi)
- Hamilton Hollow Trail (0.9 mi)
- Lakeside Trail (3.5 mi)
- Lone Spring Trail (5.2 mi)
- Mossy Hill Trail (0.8 mi)
- Prairie Trail (0.3 mi)
- Turkey Hollow Trail (0.8 mi)
- Old Schoolhouse Trail (3.85 mi)

Historic Structures
- CCC and WPA bridges, group camps, a shelter, and more

to provide economic and work relief by developing parks from sub-marginal farmland near cities to give urban residents opportunities for outdoor recreation. The lands at Cuivre had been cutover and eroded, with the valleys planted with crops and the uplands grazed by cattle. Today, after decades of careful stewardship, the park is recognized as one of the most ecologically significant and biologically diverse parks in Missouri.

Two New Deal agencies, the Civilian Conservation Corps (CCC) and the Works Progress Administration, built many of the park's facilities. Camp Sherwood Forest, designed and built in cooperation with the Park and Playground Association of St. Louis, is a perfect example of the traditional New Deal group camp. Fifty-three CCC buildings and other structures still remain, most restored for use.

Cuivre River State Park, with its restored and preserved natural communities and cultural resources, is an ideal setting in which to learn the meaning of resource stewardship. One might begin with a trip along the main park roads, where the New Deal relief workers in the 1930s painstakingly constructed masonry structures to direct water flow from one side of the road to the other. Much of their engineering is now enrolled on the National Register of Historic Places.

Even the entrance to the park is special. Following a narrow corridor of public land north from Route 47, you gently withdraw from the workaday world into peaceful wooded hills and valleys. When you cross the hand-crafted triple-arched stone bridge over Little Sugar Creek, day-to-day cares seem distant. Cuivre River is a park of hope, where nature has regenerated, and people may too. *

Current River State Park

Shannon County Rd 19-D at Hwy 19, Salem

The richly diverse park has almost two miles of Current River frontage and a superb trail network.

839 acres
Shannon County

Trails
- Centennial Bluff Trail (1.4 mi)
- Current River Trail (5.25 mi)
- Jones Hollow (4 mi)
- Winebark Trail (2.6 mi)

Historic Structures
- 1930s Alton Club Lodge, gymnasium, and dining facilities
- 20 rustic buildings

WITH THE CREATION of the Ozark National Scenic Riverways, the state had transferred most of its land on the Current River to the National Park Service. But it regained riverfront property in 2008 when the Alton Club—just upstream from Round Spring—came into the state park system.

The Alton Box Board Company began construction of its retreat in the 1930s. The buildings reflect the rustic architectural style made popular by the National Park Service early in the twentieth century. The Alton Club included man-made lakes, a lodge, barracks for both men and women, a gymnasium, pool hall, and a boathouse. As one of the few remaining intact examples of the private corporate retreats once found along the banks of the Current and Jacks Fork Rivers, it is listed in the National Register of Historic Places.

The park preserves wooded terrain steeply carved through four hundred feet of vertical relief from Route 19 to the river. The hillsides are heavily mantled in oak with numerous small dolomite glades, springs, seeps, fens, rock outcrops, bluffs, and bottomland forests. The spring-fed Current River and its tributaries are remarkably clear with abundant riffle and bluff pool habitats. With its astounding biodiversity and geological features, the park is a unique jewel among Missouri's parks. ✳

Top: This park offers ridges with memorable views of the Current River, seen here through an ancient cedar. *Ken McCarty* • Middle: A lake house at the Alton Club appears to be suspended above a man-made lake. *Ben Nickelson* • Bottom: Clear-water streams grace steep hollows on their way to the Current. *Ken McCarty*

Deutschheim State Historic Site

101 W 2nd St, Hermann

THE LOWER MISSOURI RIVER VALLEY was a beacon, promoted as a second Germany to thousands of immigrants seeking economic, intellectual, religious, or political freedom. The result was the most intense immigration movement in the history of the state. By 1860, more than half of Missouri's diverse foreign-born residents were German. Some towns like Hermann, founded in 1838, were conscious efforts to re-create all they held most dear from German towns left far behind. The region from St. Louis to Boonville along the Missouri had become a true Deutschheim or German home by the mid-nineteenth century.

Today, Hermann maintains much of the look and charm of a nineteenth-century German river town. Its well-maintained historic district and seasonal events like the Maifest, Oktoberfest, and Kristkindl Markt, along with its wineries, attract many visitors.

Deutschheim State Historic Site began with the Pommer-Gentner house and the Strehly house. Of the two historic buildings on the tour of the Deutschheim historic site, the Pommer-Gentner house is the earlier, built in 1840 for the family of Caroline Pommer, widow of Charles Pommer, piano maker and one of the organizers of the Philadelphia settlement society, who died prior to the move. It is a sterling example of German neoclassicism, featuring Beidermeier furnishings appropriate for this leading family. After a succession of other owners from 1856 to 1882, the house came into the possession of G. Henry Gentner and his wife, who had arrived in Hermann in December 1837, four months before the town was even platted. Arriving as newlyweds with few resources, the Gentners raised their family and prospered on a farm southwest of town in the intervening years.

The Strehly house, on the other hand, is a fine example of German vernacular architecture. It was built over a period of twenty-seven years, beginning about 1842. The core of the modest house—a single story and a half with a deep front porch facing the street in the European tradition—was built by Andreas Doldt. Carl Procopius Strehly of Cincinnati then acquired it in 1843. The house had a stone lower level where Strehly and his brother-in-law and business partner Eduard Muehl operated a full-service printing business; this level opened to the rear on the south-facing hillside where the partners also cultivated grapes.

The partners published two of the earliest German language newspapers west of the Mississippi, and the site has acquired and displays a printing press similar to what they would have used to publish their papers.

This stately neoclassical home was built in 1840 for the family of Caroline Pommer, widow of one of the organizers of the German Settlement Society of Philadelphia, which platted the colony at Hermann in 1840. It was the first two-story brick house in Hermann and the finest house in town. *Nick Decker*

The Strehly house has undergone major conservation and restoration. With its full printing setup, winery, and other furnishings, it provides an extraordinary window into the daily life of a German middle-class family of limited means in the 1860 to 1885 era. The Pommer-Gentner house has been restored to reflect a somewhat wealthier family in the earlier settlement period of the 1830s and 1840s. A half-timbered barn behind the house displays gardening and other tools from the nineteenth century. Period gardens, including a German four-square *gemüsegarten* (kitchen garden) at the rear of the house, offer a lovely place to stroll and to view the Missouri River.

You may also visit the Historic Hermann Museum at the German School (circa 1871) and stroll through the rest of Hermann. A visit to Deutschheim State Historic Site offers a glimpse into the lives and businesses of several founding families of Hermann, but it also illuminates Missouri's widespread German heritage. ∗

Hermann was set up as a joint-stock company. Members bought stock that entitled them to land or that could be held for profits derived from the colony.

1 acre
Gasconade County

Dillard Mill
State Historic Site

142 Dillard Mill Rd, Davisville

NESTLED AMONG THE OZARK HILLS along a rocky stretch of Huzzah Creek is one of the state's most picturesque gristmills. Dillard Mill was added to the state park system through a donated lease from the L-A-D Foundation, a private land preservation organization, in 1975. State park officials undertook a massive overhaul of the mill's mechanical systems, and today the machinery—almost all of which is original to the mill—is in good working order. Visitors delight in the creaks and moans as the turbine begins to spin, belts move, and the mill inches its way slowly back to life.

The setting of this mill is extraordinary. There are two ponds, one upstream and one downstream of the of the mill, separated by a narrow outcrop of rugged dolomite that continues to the east and south as a pine-covered bluff. As the bluff peters out, the small tributary Indian Creek enters Huzzah Creek.

The present mill was completed in 1908 by Emil Mischke, a German-Polish immigrant. He took a job at Sligo in 1899, bought the mill property, moved there in 1901 to operate a sawmill, and then built the new gristmill. The turbine used to power the mill was considered state-of-the-art next to the old waterwheel system, which was once employed here.

Today visitors can tour the fully operational mill for a nominal fee at Dillard Mill State Historic Site. You can also see the first store and post office built around 1899 by Jacob Adams. Klemme's Old Mill Lodge and several other historic buildings are used as staff residences and offices. The site also has a day-use picnic area with a shelter and a mile-and-a-half hiking trail through a glade and wooded uplands east of the mill. The trail affords a scenic overview of the mill and its ponds. The park is bordered on the east and north by Mark Twain National Forest. To a greater extent than perhaps any other mill in the state, Dillard Mill still functions as a community center.

Dillard Mill reminds us of a bygone era, when man and nature cooperated to produce one of society's needs. Of more than 900 mills that once dotted Missouri's landscape, the sites of only about 150 are known today. Some are used as houses or businesses, but all hark back to a simpler time. Along with other mills preserved in Missouri state parks, Dillard Mill is a treasure. ✳

In 1980 a millwright came to inspect the machinery. He found the mill exactly as the previous owners had left it, with all the machinery intact.

132 acres
Crawford County

Trail
• Mill View Trail (1.5 mi)

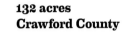

Top: The old mill stands especially picturesque on foggy fall mornings. *Phil Kamp* • Middle: Huzzah Creek flows from the southeast to Dillard along a dolomite bluff before spilling over a milldam or being channeled through the millrace. Bottom: Power from the turbine is transmitted to the mill machinery through a pair of main bevel gears made from circular iron frames. *Both Susan Flader*

Gov. Daniel Dunklin's Grave State Historic Site

Dunklin Dr, Herculaneum

President Andrew Jackson offered Dunklin the position of US surveyor general for Missouri, Illinois, and Arkansas, which he accepted with just three months remaining in his term as governor. A Bootheel county now bears his name.

1 acre
Jefferson County

ON A HIGH BLUFF overlooking the Mississippi River about a mile north of the town of Herculaneum lies the final resting place of Missouri's fifth governor. Daniel Dunklin (1790-1844) was born in South Carolina, but the pioneer spirit led him to journey west: first to Kentucky, next to Ste. Genevieve, and then to the lead belt in the vicinity of Potosi, where he pursued farming and mining interests. During the War of 1812 he joined the command of Gen. Henry Dodge in Missouri and Illinois territories. In 1815 he married a Kentucky girl named Emily Haley and opened a tavern in Potosi; he also served for four years as the Washington County sheriff. It was at his tavern in 1822 that Dunklin was nominated to the Missouri legislature as a Jacksonian Democrat.

Dunklin was elected governor in 1832. A progressive, he championed public education, humane treatment of prisoners, and a state institution for people with hearing and speech disabilities. In 1834 he recommended a state university be founded and supported by the sale of land.

The small site that serves as his resting place can be a challenge to reach in the labyrinth of subdivisions south of St. Louis, but in addition to its historical associations, it offers a superb view of the Mississippi, some three hundred feet below. *

Gov. Daniel Dunklin lies between his daughter's and son's graves. The small, one-acre family burial plot sits high on a bluff above the Mississippi River at Herculaneum and offers visitors a lovely view for quiet reflection. *Missouri State Parks and Oliver Schuchard (bottom)*

Echo Bluff State Park

35244 Echo Bluff Dr, Eminence

From 1929 into the 1980s, the property was operated as a summer camp called Camp Zoe. It's close to the historic district in Current River State Park and an extensive network of trails.

477 acres
Shannon County

Trails
- Painter Ridge Trail (2 mi)
- Current River Trail (5.25 mi)

ECHO BLUFF DOES ANSWER BACK if you give it a shout, even though you might prefer to sit quietly on the gravel bar and listen to the clear waters of Sinking Creek murmur through riffles at the base of the bluff, on their way to Current River downstream. The park is the perfect family-friendly base camp for exploring the wonders of the Missouri Ozarks.

Located between Salem and Eminence off Highway 19, the park is the Gateway to the Ozarks, a short drive from springs, caves, hiking trails, and the Ozark National Scenic Riverways, which protects the Current and Jacks Fork rivers. The park is in the vicinity of a variety of public and private conservation lands, including a national forest. A few of the nearby attractions include Rocky Falls, Blue Spring, Alley Spring Mill, and the Peck Ranch Conservation area, where you might see elk on a self-guided driving tour at dawn and dusk.

The park is in a scenic valley on Sinking Creek, a tributary of the Current. In addition to the lodge, there also are nine detached cabins with wood fireplaces and spacious decks and a campground with full-service RV hookups and walk-in showers.

The park was built with families in mind. An Adventure Playground has features, including seasonal

....

Left: The lodge has a stone fireplace soaring three stories high and twenty guest rooms, all with gas fireplaces and decks. Some are two-room suites. A veranda on the back overlooks Echo Bluff and Sinking Creek. Right: Sinking Creek offers floating, kayaking, fishing, and simply playing in the warm, shallow water along the gravel bar. The creek feeds into the Current River. *Both Ben Nickelson*

water attractions, aimed at making its young visitors comfortable when they venture into the woods. Instead of the traditional slides, swings, and sandboxes, features are designed to reflect nature. There are rocks and tree-like structures to climb. An amphitheater for nature programs and entertainment is also next to the lake.

There are two hiking trails. The Painter Ridge Trail is a two-mile loop along the bluff overlooking the park; the Current River Trail runs five miles through forested ridges high above the river valley to the adjacent Current River State Park. Mountain bikers may use the Painter Ridge Trail, which runs along the bluffs and goes by scenic glades. It begins and ends near the Blufftop Pavilion.

The park also has a general store and the Creekside Grill, which offers indoor and outdoor seating. The restaurant offers healthy choices as well as flavors of the region, local wines, and Missouri artisan-crafted beers. Picnic baskets can be pre-ordered.

The lodge also has four rooms for special events or meetings, one holding more than a hundred, as well as group outdoor settings.

But the main highlight for both children and their parents is the mile or so of Sinking Creek as it winds through the park. The creek is a short walk from the lodge. Sinking Creek is shallow and warmer than most Ozark streams, making it an enjoyable spot for wading and a gravel-bar picnic. The creek is calm but can make for a sporty float trip when waters are right. It also boasts fine smallmouth bass fishing. *

Elephant Rocks State Park

7406 Hwy 21, Belleview

A VERITABLE GEOLOGICAL CLASSROOM can be found at Elephant Rocks State Park. Here the visitor can see and touch some of the oldest rocks on the earth's surface. Here one can learn how even the hardest rocks remain at the mercy of the elements. And here one can contemplate the origin of the "elephants," the Ozarks, and the earth itself.

These pachyderms remain fascinating despite the fact that the geologic explanation puts to rest more fanciful theories of their origin. The elephants were not moved here, either by giants or by glaciers. Glaciers can carry boulders and leave them behind as the glaciers retreat—such boulders are called erratics—but the glaciers never reached as far south as the St. Francois Mountains. No, the elephants were formed right where they stand—residual boulders resisting the elements, and the product of both uplift and erosion. At Elephant Rocks State Park in Iron County, one can see all the various stages in the formation and weathering of boulders. The largest, which some know as Dumbo, leader of the herd, stands some twenty-seven feet tall and weighs an estimated 680 tons.

Missourians have been clambering around on the elephant rocks since long before the area became a state park, stretching back to the earliest white settlers, and probably Native Americans before them. By the 1870s, St. Louis artists were producing "views of the elephants," and the beloved old weathered boulders were the inspiration for the lifelike settings developed to house and display the hoofed animals at the St. Louis Zoo, built as a part of the 1904 World's Fair.

The area was suggested for a state park in 1924, but fourteen years later when Secretary of the Interior Harold Ickes came to Missouri to dedicate Babler Memorial State Park near St. Louis, he lamented, "Years ago this state should have set aside the Elephant Rocks, which have now been hammered to pieces." Fortunately, he was not entirely correct, and in 1967 a remnant of the site came into the state park system.

But it is the rocks that beckon, urging you to experience the joy of exploring or to ponder their origins. Here, among the ancient boulders of Elephant Rocks State Park, you can lose yourself in the weathered maze and ponder that you're standing in the very core of the Ozarks. *

Top: You can see how Elephant Rocks State Park got its name. *Paul Nelson* • Middle: From the high rocks, you can view the deceptively flat horizon of the Ozarks. *David Stoner* • Bottom: Geologists tell us the red granite is about 1.5 billion years old. *Jim Smith*

The "elephants" were formed by magma cooling into granite under the earth's surface, and then brought up by erosion, weathering, and upward movement caused by the earth's plates. Someday more of these rocks may come to surface by the same processes.

**149 acres
Iron County**

Trails
- Braille Trail (1 mi)
- Engine House Ruins Trail (0.4 mi)

Historic Structures
- Engine House ruins
- quarries

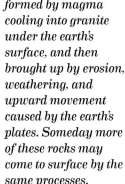

Eleven Point State Park

Rt Y Southeast of Alton

The large house on what was known as the Pigman Ranch hosted the Beatles during a break from their 1964 tour of America. The house's exterior displays the Ozark style called "giraffe" because the irregular sandstone resembles that animal's hide.

**4,167 acres
Oregon County**

THE NATIONAL WILD AND SCENIC River System was created by Congress in 1968 to preserve rivers with outstanding natural, cultural, and recreational values. The Eleven Point River in southeast Missouri was among the first on the list.

The new Eleven Point State Park includes six miles of frontage on the river, where the US Forest Service maintains the wild and scenic character that earned it national recognition. Because it is spring fed, the river features the clear, cold water that characterizes the best of the famed Ozarks' floating streams.

The state park, includes more than 3,000 acres of native woodlands and forest, 14 tributary streams and several springs, and nearly 1,000 acres of open uplands or pasture. The fields have been heavily grazed, and prescribed burns may be used to bring back the natural landscape of grasses and wildflowers beneath open woodlands of scattered post oaks.

Visitors could put in canoes or kayaks at the access at Riverton and float alongside the park nine miles to the Highway 142 access, which is known as The Narrows. It's a quiet stretch with solitude. That's saying something on our Ozark rivers. ＊

Top: The park includes frontage on the Eleven Point River, with beautiful views of forested river hills and bluffs overlooking the national wild and scenic river corridor. *Missouri State Parks* • Bottom: The site of this future park includes a house where the Beatles stayed during a break from their 1964 tour of America. *Tom Uhlenbrock*

Finger Lakes State Park

1505 E Peabody Rd, Columbia

THIS MAN-MADE LANDSCAPE is probably not recognized as such at this park just north of Columbia. A half-century has passed since the Peabody Coal Company shovels ripped up soil and rock to reach the coal below. Since then, there has been some recovery, both from natural seeding and from human-assisted replanting. Still, the rugged terrain—steep ridges and deep ravines, many of which are water-filled—is the telltale aftermath of a resource-extraction process known simply as strip mining.

Coal has always been one of Missouri's most abundant resources, and coal mining has been an important industry here, even though it is also followed by controversy. The state ranks among the top ten in quantity of coal reserves.

In just a little more than three years, beginning in 1964, the Peabody Company removed some 1.2 million tons of coal from its Mark Twain Mine. After ceasing mining, Peabody undertook some initial reclamation, planting the barren piles of waste and stocking some water-filled pits as fishing lakes.

In the early 1970s, the US Department of the Interior initiated a program to recycle strip-mine areas as "reclamation for recreation" demonstration projects. The State Park Board identified the Mark Twain Mine as a good candidate. The Peabody Company agreed in 1973 to donate about one thousand acres to the state of Missouri, a donation that was matched with funds for development from the federal Land and Water Conservation Fund. At Finger Lakes, the emphasis would be on reconfiguring the topography and reclaiming the lands for off-road motorcycling and water recreation.

Finger Lakes will never be a natural area, but it is

a real success as a recreation area. Peabody Lake, one of the larger lakes, was developed with a sand swimming beach and a changing house. Several of the finger-shaped pits in the eastern half of the park were connected to form a canoe trail nearly five miles long where the fishing is good and visitors have a chance of spotting great blue herons, beavers, raccoons, or deer. There is a boat launch area, and the park now rents canoes and kayaks. A pleasant tree-shaded campground has been developed at the north end of the park.

But the real measure of the park's popularity lies in its use for off-road vehicles (ORVs): four-wheel vehicles with handlebars also known as all-terrain-vehicles (ATVs) and dirt bikes. There is a five-mile designated, marked, and maintained trail from the campground to the motocross track, the staging area, and south to the park office, but ORV users have pioneered some seventy miles of challenging routes across the steep hills and ravines of the strip-mined spoil area.

The motocross track, developed by professional riders and park planners, is close to Highway 63 in the western part of the park. This area hosts special events each year, co-sponsored by the park and outside organizations. The event draws both professional and amateur riders from across the country. The park also features the only bicycle "pump track" in a Missouri state park. This concrete oval with eight bumps or "pumps" requires riders to use an up and down pumping motion to propel their bike forward without pedaling. A twelve-piece skills course also lets mountain bikers practice. *

This drone view from above the park center shows the finger-shaped lakes to the south—and how the park got its name. *Paul Jackson*

The park represents a creative recycling of strip-mined land for recreational use, attracting off-roaders who coexist well with those who prefer fishing, swimming, kayaking, bicycling and hiking.

1,138 acres
Boone County

Trails

- Kelley Branch Mountain Bike Trail (2.4 mi)
- ORV Main Trail (5.25 mi)
- Finger Lakes State Park Water Trail (4.5 mi)

First Missouri State Capitol
State Historic Site

200 S Main St, St Charles

Four Missouri governors ran the state's affairs from the capitol in St. Charles in the five-year period it served as the state's temporary capital.

1 acre
St. Charles County

SIMPLE FEDERAL-STYLE, two-story brick row houses were the home to Missouri's first capitol complex on South Main Street in St. Charles. Originally built in 1818 for commercial and residential purposes, the structures achieved their greatest fame as the seat of Missouri government for five years from 1821 to 1826.

At least nine towns competed for the honor of being the temporary capital city. Ultimately, St. Charles—a city of about a thousand people with excellent access to the most rapidly growing areas of the state both by river and overland via the Boone's Lick Road—was selected for its conspicuous advantages.

The buildings selected as the capitol were owned by the Peck brothers, Charles and Ruluff, who operated a general store and lived on the first floor of the south building. The senate and the "room" of representatives, as well as Gov. Alexander McNair's office, were upstairs. Today, all these rooms have been restored to reflect the 1821 to 1826 period.

Today, Main Street in front of the capitol and Frontier Park and Katy Trail State Park behind it attract visitors to the site daily, making it one of the most heavily visited sites in Missouri. Just as the first state capitol brought a flurry of activity to the young town on the Missouri River, so too did its restoration spark the continuing economic revival of old St. Charles. ✳

Top: A drone camera captures the capitol with Frontier Park, the Katy Trail, and the Missouri River just beyond. St. Charles provided access by river and overland to growing parts of the state. *Paul Jackson* • Bottom: The building's second floor housed Missouri's first General Assembly and governor's office. *Tom Nagel*

Graham Cave State Park

217 Hwy TT, Danville

ABOVE THE LOUTRE RIVER in the hills a few miles north of the Loutre's confluence with the Missouri River is an outcrop with a large cave created at the contact zone between St. Peter sandstone and Jefferson City dolomite. Caves in dolomite or limestone are common enough, but a sandstone cave is less common. What is noteworthy, though, is not so much the cave, rare as it is, as what has been found in the debris on its floor. This cave, like others so favorably situated, was an admirable shelter for animals and people through the years—just how many years would one day be discovered.

Dr. Robert Graham, a Scotsman who came to Missouri from Kentucky in the wave of migration that followed the War of 1812, settled in the area in 1816 and purchased from Daniel Morgan Boone a portion of his rich bottomland along the Loutre River. In 1847, he acquired from the federal government the parcel of land containing the cave.

From 1949 through about 1955, archaeologists Wilfred Logan and Carl Chapman of the University of Missouri and the Missouri Archaeological Society conducted extensive excavations in the cave. The results were staggering. Within a deep portion of the deposits, they found evidence of the oldest known humans in Missouri up to that time. These discoveries were being made just as the new carbon-14 technology for dating organic material such as bone or wood was substantially revising archaeologists' notions of when early people had arrived on the continent. It had once been thought that they had arrived less than three thousand years ago, but discoveries in New Mexico were forcing scientists to push their estimates backward. The hard evidence came with radiocarbon dating at places like Graham Cave. Today, a visitors center displays artifacts from the excavations and tells the story of the natives and the landscape they inhabited for nearly ten thousand years.

The extremely significant discoveries at Graham Cave, including not only the oldest materials but also the remarkable evidence of ways of life and adaptations to the environment over ten millennia, were recognized when Frances Graham Darnell took pride in the discoveries made on her land and donated 237 acres—land that had been in her family for nearly a century and a half—to the state in 1964. *

Top: Archaeologists have found that the cave has had almost continuous human habitation over the last ten thousand years. *Ben Nickelson* • Middle: Visitors explore a sandstone bluff. Bottom: Five trails explore different areas ranging from bottomland forest to glades and open oak woodlands. *Both Missouri State Parks*

NATIONAL HISTORIC LANDMARK

In November 1961, Graham Cave became the first archaeological site in the nation to be designated a National Historic Landmark.

386 acres Montgomery County

Trails
- Fern Ridge Trail (0.3 mi)
- Graham Cave Trail (0.3 mi)
- Indian Glade Trail (0.9)
- Lourtre River (2.5 mi)
- Woodland Way (0.2 mi)

Grand Gulf State Park

Rt W, Thayer

Grand Gulf features a collapsed cave system stretching for nearly three-quarters of a mile. *Missouri State Parks*

LOCAL OLD-TIMERS KNEW IT all along. The stream of Grand Gulf canyon a few miles north of the Missouri-Arkansas line, which disappears into subterranean caverns, reemerges nine miles south as the famous Mammoth Spring that bursts from the earth in Arkansas. In 1941, folklorist Otto Rayburn reported a local experiment: people dumped sacks of oats into the stream in the canyon and then observed the oats emerge in the spring. Later investigators confirmed the experiment with fluorescein dye.

All of this water flowing through Grand Gulf's striking landscape still today passes through a 250-foot natural tunnel—the part of the cave that remains intact—and emerges into a large circular chasm. Here the stream submerges back into the cave system and begins its Stygian journey toward Mammoth Spring.

The steep walls here, rising as high as 130 feet, required explorers to make their way upstream for some distance to gain safe access. Then, walking downstream, they could enter the tunnel, which at ordinary water levels is some seventy-five feet high. If they happened to notice that the flood debris had reached this same height, they'd have known to scan the sky for possible thunderheads before proceeding. The ceiling height drops to only about ten feet on the downstream end of the tunnel.

This passage from the chasm to the cave long fascinated scientists and spelunkers. How could so massive a cave system pinch out into such a small, unimpressive end? Accounts by earlier explorers give the answer. In her now classic *Cave Regions of the Ozarks and Black Hills* (1898), the young scientist Luella Agnes Owen recounted her exploration along with two companions. She described what they saw after entering the cave at the downstream end of the gulf and proceeding perhaps six hundred feet farther downstream: "The ceiling dipped so we were not able to stand straight, and the guide said he had never gone farther; but to his surprise here was a light boat, which I am ready to admit, he displayed no eagerness to appropriate to his own use, and swimming about it, close to shore, were numerous small, eyeless fish, pure white and perfectly fearless; the first I had ever seen, and little beauties."

Luella determined to use the boat to explore the underground stream even further, leaving her nephew and the guide behind holding a coil of slender twine that would be her only lifeline to return against the current. Luella continued in the boat along a narrow, rocky channel until she came to an even smaller passage where she could lodge the boat sideways against the rocks. Then, acceding to the shouts of her guide that he feared the twine could be severed by the rocks, she let him pull her back.

Access to the first part of the cave was available, according to local residents, until the early 1920s when a great storm filled the gulf with downed trees and other debris. In the 1990s, state park officials employed a robot that toted a camera and digging tool to try to find a way past the flood debris and into the cave. They eventually gave up, deciding that any effort to break up the plug could risk havoc at Mammoth Spring and the adjacent town during floods.

Today, park managers have laid out trails and installed a wheelchair-accessible overlook at this day-use park, so some sixty thousand visitors a year can get close to the edge of the gulf without endangering themselves or the environment. A hike on the mile-long woodland trail surrounding the gulf reveals evidence of debris that has floated along the shorelines, indicating high-water marks. Outdoor exhibits at the trailhead illustrate the geology, so visitors can visualize the processes that produced Missouri's "Little Grand Canyon." *

Heavy rains can fill the entire gulf to depths exceeding one hundred feet. Several times in recent years, even the 130-foot-high observation platform has been covered.

322 acres
Oregon County

Trails
- Interpretive Loop Trail (0.25 mi)
- Natural Bridge Trail (0.8 mi)

Ha Ha Tonka State Park

1491 State Rd D, Camdenton

NEARLY SEVENTY YEARS PASSED after Ha Ha Tonka was initially proposed as a park before it was finally acquired by the state. Gov. Herbert S. Hadley recommended it to become Missouri's first state park in 1909, but the property changed hands frequently, with many owners failing to realize their development dreams. As one St. Louis realtor and conservationist pointed out, the tract seemed cursed. In 1978, the curse was broken, and Ha Ha Tonka became Missouri's sixty-first state park.

High on a bluff overlooking the spring and the Niangua River—now the Niangua arm of Lake of the Ozarks—are the ruins of a massive stone mansion and its companion structures. These ruins represent what is probably the most intriguing episode in Ha Ha Tonka's fascinating history. They also represent the origin of the supposed curse.

Robert M. Snyder, a wealthy businessman from Kansas City, first visited the area in 1903 on a hunting trip. He stayed at a hotel in nearby Lebanon, where he learned about the wonders of Ha Ha Tonka. Immediately captivated, Snyder set out to acquire some sixty different tracts of land, beginning with the tract that included the spring and eventually totaling more than five thousand acres. He envisioned a private retreat with a huge, European-style castle. With native stone quarried on the site and stonemasons from Scotland, the 85-by-115-foot structure began taking shape in 1905. In addition, an 80-foot-high

3,752 acres
Camden County

Trails

- Acorn Trail (0.9 mi)
- Boulder Ridge (1.5 mi)
- Castle Trail (0.4 mi)
- Cedar Trail (0.2 mi)
- Colosseum Trail (0.7 mi)
- Dell Rim (0.3 mi)
- Devil's Kitchen Trail (1.25 mi)
- Dolomite Rock Trail (2.5 mi)
- Island Trail (0.8 mi)
- Lake Trail (0.4 mi)
- Oak Woodland Interpretive Trail (0.08 mi)
- Quarry Trail (1.75 mi)
- Spring Trail (1.5 mi)
- Turkey Pen Hollow Trail (6.5 mi)

stone water tower was constructed, and greenhouses and stables were designed and begun.

But in 1906, Snyder was killed in an automobile accident. All work at Ha Ha Tonka ceased, and the fate of the place was in doubt. Eventually, Snyder's sons finished the castle, though not to their father's sumptuous specifications. And tragedy struck again in 1942 when the wooden shingles on the roof of this supposedly fireproof building caught fire and the entire interior was gutted. The crumbling stone walls have maintained a lonely vigil ever since.

Since acquiring the land, the park division has invested nearly a million dollars in virtually invisible stabilization of the castle ruins so beloved by visitors, to prevent them from tumbling into a pile of rubble. Park designers and estate planners in the nineteenth century went to considerable lengths to deliberately create false ruins in the landscape, so it is not surprising that Missourians should want to preserve the real ones so spectacularly situated at Ha Ha Tonka.

The park is Missouri's premiere showcase of karst geology. Trails and boardwalks make it easy for visitors to see the honeycomb of tunnels, caverns, spring, and sinkholes. A large relief map carved from stone at a small open-air information pavilion shows these remarkable geologic features. The park is also one of Missouri's best examples of a woodland landscape. More than four hundred plant species have been recorded here, and wildflower displays change throughout the seasons. A large section is protected as the Ha Ha Tonka Oak Woodland Natural Area.

Ha Ha Tonka is a popular park, with more than half a million visitors annually. The park is a wonderland that won't disappoint. ∗

Left: Ha Ha Tonka Spring, the state's twelfth largest, may be viewed from a boardwalk overlook. Randal Clark • Right: The scenic grandeur and the castle saga are only part of the park's appeal. In a single square mile, the park contains caves, springs, chasms, sinkholes, underground streams, and natural bridges. Tom Nagel

Hawn is the only state park where you can find the fragrant rose azalea. The Whispering Pine Wild Area offers more than fifteen miles of interconnected loop trails. Hikers like the changing landscapes: terraced cliffs covered with ferns and moss, miniature terrarium-like gardens overhanging rock shelves along clear streams, distant pine-clad hills, and uplands broken by boulders and exposed bedrock.

**4,956 acres
Ste. Genevieve County**

Trails
- Pickle Creek Trail (0.7 mi)
- Overlook Trail (300 ft)
- Whispering Pines Trail (9.75 mi)
- White Oaks Trail (3.75 mi)

Hawn State Park

12096 Park Dr, Ste. Genevieve

THERE IS ONLY ONE WAY to really take in the pleasures of Hawn State Park, and that is by foot. True, the campgrounds and picnic areas are accessible by automobile. But to see the bulk of this park and to savor its riches, you must strike out across the sandy forest floor, strewn with pine needles.

Hawn State Park preserves Missouri's most exemplary concentration of distinctive Lamotte sandstone landscape features. Its sculpted outcrops provide a contrast to the more usual dolomites and limestones that poke through most of Missouri's landscape. The park's principal streams, Pickle Creek and River aux Vases, have carved steep-sided ravines into the thick beds of the Lamotte, reaching the more erosion-resistant igneous rock and creating shut-ins.

The unique ability of this sandstone to hold moisture and produce acidic soils allows for distinctive flora. Mixed pine and hardwood forest in some areas give way to pure stands of mature shortleaf pine. Parts of the park have a forest floor literally carpeted with needles over the whitish sands of the Lamotte.

In a few remote corners of the park, the erosive action of water on sandstone has produced box canyons that are cooler, damper, and shadier than the surrounding hillsides. These microhabitats provide refuge for animals and plants usually found in more northern states, such as many species of fern, including the rare hay-scented fern and spinulose shield fern. The beautiful showy orchids and other orchids are abundant, including the rare green adder's mouth and rattlesnake plantain orchid. Other relicts include partridgeberry and Canadian white violet.

Even the creeks are special. Pickle Creek, with its clear water, sandy bottom, shaded surface, and lack of much aquatic vegetation, supports at least twenty species of fish: various minnows, darters, and shiners, even an occasional smallmouth bass. Nearly sixty acres along it comprise the Pickle Creek Natural Area.

If you hike about a mile south from the campground, the trail leads up a remnant erosional knob of sandstone called Evans Knob. You're only about three hundred feet above Pickle Creek and not that far from the park comfort station, but standing there in that old forest—mostly white oak, shortleaf pine, and scarlet oak with a sprinkling of flowering dogwood and wild blueberry—you feel transported back in time before this remote, rugged terrain was settled. This is the magic of Hawn State Park. *

Top: The 2,880-acre Whispering Pine Wild Area offers more than fifteen miles of connected loop trails. *Ron Colatskie* • Bottom: Pickle Creek cascades through shut-ins formed by erosion-resistant granite in the Pickle Creek Natural Area. *Missouri State Parks*

Hunter-Dawson
State Historic Site

312 Dawson Rd, New Madrid

This home reminds us that Missouri, a border state with mostly upper South historical connections, also has ties with the deeper Delta South. Tree species typical of the Bootheel dot the twenty-acre site.

**20 acres
New Madrid
County**

CONSTRUCTION BEGAN IN 1859 on this fifteen-room mansion, by William Washington Hunter, a fifty-two-year-old Bootheel businessman. Although Hunter died before the house was completed, his widow, Amanda Watson Hunter, moved in with seven of her nine children just before the Civil War. After his death, Amanda, her sons, and her brother continued to run the store, a gristmill, and a lumber mill. In 1876, the house passed to their daughter Ella and her husband of two years, William W. Dawson. Descendants of the Hunter family occupied the house until 1958. In 1966, the city of New Madrid bought the house and donated it to the state a year later.

The frame house was built by Hunter's slaves and hired craftsmen and features bald cypress lumber from nearby swamp forests. It displays traces of Georgian, Greek Revival, and Italianate architecture. The collection of original furniture includes the largest collection of Mitchell and Rammelsburg furniture that still exists in its original location.

A bare-bones summation can scarcely suggest the manifold connections these remarkable families had with the settlement and development of the Mississippi Lowlands from Spanish times to our own. The beautifully restored Hunter-Dawson home reflects their success. ✳

Top: The families who lived in this antebellum home helped transform the Mississippi Lowlands. *Missouri State Parks* • Middle: Many furnishings, like this full-canopy bed, are original to the home and were still in the home when it became a state historic site. *Brian Sirimaturos* • Bottom: The table is also original to the house, which has nine fireplaces. *Missouri State Parks*

Iliniwek Village State Historic Site

Rt 27, Wayland

IN THE SEVENTEENTH CENTURY when France had an empire in the interior of North America, there was a large region in the center of the continent known to the French as *Le pays des Illinois*, "The Illinois Country." It was a deferential nod to those whose country it was, the dozen or so American Indian tribes of the Illinois Confederation who occupied this vast region that encompassed most of the middle Mississippi valley from Iowa to Arkansas.

Of course, "Illinois" is a transcription by early French explorers of a Native American term; today, we know a more nearly correct spelling is "Iliniwek." This Algonquin-related word was used by other Indians to refer to the allied tribes of the Confederation. The meaning of the word "Iliniwek" was that the members of those tribes all spoke a common language that was mutually understood, but the word that the Iliniwek used to refer to themselves was "Inoka," most likely meaning "the people."

In his time, Father Jacques Marquette was particularly stirred by the stories he heard from visiting Iliniwek, stories of a great river, "Missisipi" (Marquette's spelling), and of large Iliniwek villages along it, one of which more than three centuries later would become Iliniwek Village State Historic Site in far northeast Missouri.

On the morning of May 17, 1673, Father Marquette, Louis Jolliet (also spelled Joliet), and their companions left the mission of St. Ignace at the Straits of Mackinac in Michigan and headed south-west, Father Marquette in hope of harvesting Iliniwek souls and Jolliet in search of glory—or at the very least, value for his king and country.

On June 25, 1673, while traveling down the Mississippi, they saw a path made by humans along the riverbank near the mouth of a tributary. Leaving their canoes and crew behind, Marquette and Jolliet cautiously followed the path alone on foot. A half-dozen miles inland from the Mississippi along the channel of the Des Moines River, they saw a village, actually a complex of three villages with a total of three hundred dwellings and several thousand Indians. The explorers stood in surprise, watching the village scene until a group of four elderly men walked out to them, bringing the calumet, or peace pipe, in welcome.

For the next three hundred years, no one knew where this village had been. Then in 1984 a routine archaeological survey for a rural waterline found it, not in Iowa as had been thought, but here in Missouri.

Today, the historic site offers tables for picnics and a kiosk featuring attractive graphic panels explaining the Iliniwek and their way of life at the village. Altogether there is a little more than a mile of trail, leading to several areas where archaeological excavations have taken place and to the oxbow lake. Along the trail, visitors may see the outlines on the ground of two of the Iliniwek structures. As archaeologists uncovered the traces of the original side posts of the houses, new posts were installed into the old postholes, resulting in physical outlines of the houses on the ground.

The Iliniwek Village State Historic Site is a reminder of the vagaries of history and of a time when our part of the world was once part of someone else's world, *Le pays des Illinois*. *

Today, most of the sand prairie in the state, including on the Des Moines River terraces, has been plowed under and turned to cropland. But a few scattered small tracts have survived, and the Iliniwek Village State Historic Site is one.

**128 acres
Clark County**

Trail
- Oxbow Trail (1.25 mi)

Left: Plains puccoon flourishes on a sand prairie, a rare natural community here in Missouri. *Bruce Schuette* • Right: The posts mark an Iliniwek round house next to the Oxbow Trail. *Missouri State Parks*

Jewell Cemetery State Historic Site

S Providence Rd, Columbia

SOUTH OF DOWNTOWN COLUMBIA is a small cemetery where Missouri's twenty-second governor is buried, as is the founder of William Jewell College. Bordered by a low stone wall with an iron gate, the cemetery was once part of the estate of George Jewell, who founded one of Missouri's early dynasties. In 1841, he deeded the cemetery to his son William and grandson Thomas. More than forty descendants of George Jewell are buried there, the most noteworthy being William Jewell, patron of many colleges, including the one named for him at Liberty, and Gov. Charles Hardin.

Jewell Cemetery is a remnant of the nineteenth century amid the modern sprawl of south Columbia. Within its stone walls, the site retains its integrity. The earliest grave dates from 1822, and the most recent from 1968. At the back of the cemetery are about twenty unlettered but neatly quarried blocks of native limestone, thought to be markers for the graves of slaves or former slaves of the Jewell family. William Jewell freed some of his slaves in 1836 and the remainder upon his death in 1852. If these are slave graves, they represent an unusual exception to traditional nineteenth-century practices, as slaves were usually not buried inside walled-in family enclosures. *

The state legislature in 1967 mandated the State Park Board to "suitably mark and maintain every grave of a former governor of this state, which is not in a perpetual care cemetery."

1 acre
Boone County

Top: This family plot in Columbia contains more than forty descendants of George Jewell, including former governor Charles Hardin. A plaque reminds visitors that only Jewell kin are to be buried here. *Annie Rice* • Bottom: William Jewell was a physician, politician, minister, architect, and patron of many colleges, including the one named for him and which he founded in Liberty. *Missouri State Parks*

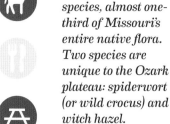

Johnson's Shut-Ins State Park

148 Taum Sauk Trail, Middle Brook

This park is home to more than 900 plant species, almost one-third of Missouri's entire native flora. Two species are unique to the Ozark plateau: spiderwort (or wild crocus) and witch hazel.

9,432 acres
Reynolds County

Trails
- Black River Trail System (3.15 mi)
- Campground Trail System (3 mi)
- Goggins Mountain Equestraian Trail (10 mi)
- Horseshoe Glade Trail (1.5 mi)
- Scour Trail (2 mi)
- Shut-Ins Trail (2.25 mi)
- Taum Sauk section (14.5 mi) of the Ozark Trail (35 mi)

THIS PARK IS A PHOENIX, reborn of flood and wind rather than fire. Since its inception in the 1950s, Johnson's Shut-Ins in Reynolds County has been among the best-known state parks in Missouri, but the chutes and potholes of its photogenic shut-ins were ravaged by one of the more cataclysmic dam failures in American history.

On December 14, 2005, the Taum Sauk Reservoir atop nearby Proffit Mountain suddenly collapsed and in only twelve minutes sent 1.3 billion gallons of water roaring seven thousand feet down the mountainside and into the heart of the park. Then, just a few years later, the park's mountainous wild areas took a direct hit on May 8, 2009, from an extraordinarily powerful windstorm that toppled about 90 percent of the oak and pine canopy in some areas. But Johnson's Shut-Ins has already rebounded.

Located in the St. Francois Mountains at the geologic core of the Ozarks, the park is justly famed for its rocks. Pink granites, porphyries, and blue-gray rhyolites offer testimony to an era of primordial volcanism more than a billion years ago. As the East Fork of the Black River leaves the more easily eroded dolomitic bedrock of a relatively broad valley upstream of the park and meets the resistant igneous rocks of the ancient ash and lava flows in the park, the valley becomes narrow and canyon-like. Water ceaselessly finds the least resistant course. Sometimes it makes a right-angle change in direction, creating eddies and crosscurrents. The resulting gorges and rock gardens have come to be called shut-ins. These, named for homesteaders, are the most famous in the St. Francois Mountains.

Most visitors to Johnson's Shut-Ins see only a small part of the park—the visitor center, the picnic grounds, the campground, and the shut-ins overlook. The more adventurous wade, swim, and play in the swirling waters, climbing and sliding on the smooth and slippery volcanic rocks or sitting in the gravel-scoured potholes.

But the vast majority of the park is a near-wilderness welcoming hiking. Nearly three-quarters of this acreage is included in the East Fork and Goggins Mountain Wild Areas. If you should find a line for the Shut-Ins when you arrive, especially in summer, there are other places to park to walk the trails. ✳

Top: In the heat of summer, the shut-ins beckon park visitors for a cool splash. *Scott Myers* • Middle: Hikers admire the vista from the Ozark Trail. *Paul Barbercheck* • Bottom: Wild hyacinth blooms in spring and brightens Horseshoe Glade in the East Fork Wild Area. A hike here leads into igneous rock barrens. *Allison Vaughn*

Scott Joplin House State Historic Site

2658 Delmar Blvd., St. Louis

SCOTT JOPLIN WAS THE KING OF RAGTIME, and John S. Stark proclaimed him so. Between them, a composer and his publisher, they had a major hand in the direction and sound of American music in the first decades of the twentieth century.

In 1894 he was living in Sedalia, where he played cornet in the Queen City Cornet Band, led his own six-piece dance band, and still occasionally toured with the Texas Medley vocal group. But he made his mark by playing piano at the 400 Club and Maple Leaf Club, two Black social clubs in town where he continued to hone his skills in the free-flowing, improvisational, artistic expression of Black musicians from the minstrel tradition. He also attended the George R. Smith College for Negroes, learning the formal structure of classical music and accurate musical notation, so that he could record on paper the African American rhythms he had learned. Joplin eventually became the leader in a new, syncopated musical genre that was becoming a national sensation—ragtime.

Joplin's composition, the "Maple Leaf Rag," became immensely popular and boosted both Joplin and his publisher's prospects. John S. Stark had been an ice cream maker and a piano and organ salesman, and he had taken over a failing music-publishing house in Sedalia. Riding on the success of "Maple Leaf," Stark relocated the publishing company to St. Louis, and Scott Joplin soon followed.

Musical genius or not, as a Black man Joplin had limited options for housing in turn-of-the-century St. Louis. The building he moved into at 2658A Morgan, now Delmar Boulevard, had in the mid-1800s been part of a prosperous German neighborhood, but by

1900, most German families had moved to neighborhoods farther west. The house had been built as a duplex, but later the east unit had been converted into a two-flat. Joplin had moved into a bustling neighborhood of the working poor: waiters, janitors, porters, firemen, laborers, and, yes, musicians. A few of the original German families were still there, along with the most recent Irish immigrants to the city, but the district had become increasingly Black.

Today, the ground floor contains exhibits explaining the history of the house, its restoration, and the neighborhood. On the second floor of the west unit is a small archive room. On the east side are more exhibits about Joplin and his music and a room housing an authentic, operating player piano and a collection of piano rolls, some actually cut by Joplin.

Visitors can pass through an opening in the thin boarding that had enclosed the staircase and climb the stairs into a world of turn-of-the-century St. Louis. Lit with gaslights and oil lamps, the flat where Joplin lived is small, with a parlor, a bedroom, and a small kitchen. The flat is provided with period furnishings, and it seems only right that the flat has a piano, but it isn't known for certain if Joplin was able to afford his own at this time.

Today, the Scott Joplin State Historic Site attracts a variety of visitors, from local school groups learning about life and music in early 1900s St. Louis to out-of-town musical groups to syncopation aficionados, who come from across the world to pay homage to "the king of ragtime." The site includes the Rosebud Cafe, a reconstructed turn-of-the-century bar and gaming club. It also pays tribute to the creativity and talent of a gifted musician who called Missouri home, and it celebrates the many rich African American contributions to Missouri's cultural history. *

At the turn of the twentieth century, Scott Joplin moved into a second floor flat of this building. It is the last surviving structure known to have been associated with Joplin. *Peter Ciro*

"We mean to advertise these as classic rags, and we mean just what we say. They have lifted ragtime from its low estate and lined it up with Beethoven and Bach."—John Stark, Publisher

4 acres
St. Louis

Katy Trail State Park

Trailheads in many towns

The Katy runs through dense forests, lush wetlands, deep valleys, steep hills, towering bluffs, remnant prairies, open pasturelands, and gently rolling farm fields.

240 miles across 14 counties

IT'S LONG BUT ONLY 100 FEET WIDE! That's an odd shape for a state park, but that's the Katy Trail. An abandoned railroad converted into a state park, it stretches almost entirely across Missouri, sometimes squeezed in tight between towering stone bluffs on one side and the Missouri River on the other. For hikers, bicyclists, and on some stretches, equestrians, it is a path through both nature and history, leading to historic and picturesque villages and even into several larger cities, where you can find your own dining and lodging options. Of all the units in the Missouri park system, Katy Trail State Park offers the most varied mixture of cultural and natural resources.

The park was built on the former corridor of the Missouri-Kansas-Texas (MKT) Railroad, better known as the Katy. It is the longest rail-to-trail conversion out of more than 1,600 such conversions throughout the nation. Trail users travel through some of the most scenic parts of the state, through dense forest, wetlands, deep valleys, remnant prairies, open pastureland, and rolling farm fields. Although the scenery changes, the trail remains fairly level with gentle grades. Surely no other such trail can match the Katy for the historical significance and sheer magnificence of the Missouri River corridor—the pathway for the exploration and settlement of the American West. ✳

Top: Hundreds of bicyclists participate in parks-sponsored Katy Trail events. *Missouri State Park* • Bottom: The trail provides either solitary or social exercise or a 240-mile adventure exploring towns along the way. You can see some of the finest seasonal colors in the state from the seat of your bicycle. *Dennis Coello*

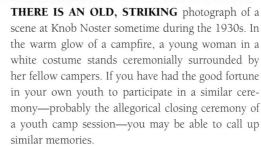

Knob Noster State Park

873 SE 10, Knob Noster

THERE IS AN OLD, STRIKING photograph of a scene at Knob Noster sometime during the 1930s. In the warm glow of a campfire, a young woman in a white costume stands ceremonially surrounded by her fellow campers. If you have had the good fortune in your own youth to participate in a similar ceremony—probably the allegorical closing ceremony of a youth camp session—you may be able to call up similar memories.

The group camps of the state parks were conceived during the Great Depression to provide the opportunity for just such experiences for youngsters who might not otherwise be able to attend a privately run camp. These camps were built mostly by labor in work relief programs, the Civilian Conservation Corps and the Works Progress Administration (WPA). The camps are for the most part still functioning today, including two—Camp Shawnee and Camp Bobwhite, built between 1938 and 1941—at Knob Noster State Park.

The WPA also built a campground and picnic area, several small lakes, and various bridges and service buildings. Many of these buildings and other structures are still intact today and are listed on the National Register of Historic Places.

This park, now nearly four thousand acres, attracts over a quarter of a million visitors a year. Its two group camps can be rented by nonprofit groups. The park has two fishing lakes and seven trails totaling nearly twenty miles, including trails for mountain biking and horses. The park has a small natural area, Pin Oak Slough, and an old oxbow of Clearfork Creek.

Come and set up your camp in the shady public campground. Enjoy some quiet fishing or kayaking in Clearfork or Buteo Lake. Take advantage of a naturalist-led program or guided walk. Bring a mountain bike to ride the Opossum Hollow Trail or your horse to ride the McAdoo Trail. Hike out to a prairie or woodland area, listen to the dickcissels calling in the tall bluestem, and imagine the old Missouri landscape. In the evening, you can enjoy your own golden campfire. The summer night still resounds with whippoorwills and barred owls. The fireflies still flicker like tiny stars, and the glow of a circle of friends or family can still create magical memories. *

Top: The lakes here offer nonmotorized boating and fishing. Middle: The Hawk's Nest Trail passes through an open woodland restored with prescribed fire, which brings out the wildflowers. *Both Scott Myers* • The Camp Fire Girls conduct a ceremony at a fire circle in the 1930s at a group camp at Knob Noster. *State Park Archives*

A young Missouri Confederate soldier, Ephraim McDowell Anderson, who marched with his companions through the Knob Noster vicinity in 1861, described the area like this: "The view opens upon boundless and beautiful prairies, dotted with clumps of trees."

3,934 acres
Johnson County

Trails
- Buteo Trail (1 mi)
- Clearfork Woodland Trail (0.6 mi)
- Discovery Trail (0.9 mi)
- Hawk Nest Trail (1.6 mi)
- McAdoo Trail System Trail (6.5 mi)
- North Loop Trail (1.8 mi)
- Opossum Trail (5.5 mi)

Historic Structures
- WPA youth camps, campground, bridges, and more

Lake of the Ozarks State Park

403 Hwy. 134, Kaiser

MISSOURI'S LARGEST and most varied park is an inheritance from the Great Depression. The farm economy was collapsing even before the historic stock market crash in 1929, the event often cited as triggering the economic decline that prostrated not only America but most of the industrialized world. Swept into the presidency by an unhappy electorate in 1932, the pragmatic and innovative Franklin D. Roosevelt quickly launched a series of programs aimed at relieving unemployment and widespread human distress.

As part of the National Industrial Recovery Act of 1933, a system of Recreational Demonstration Areas (RDAs) was authorized to test the feasibility of converting submarginal farmlands into outdoor recreation areas suitable for transfer later to the states. Beginning in 1942, they were conveyed to the states; the ones in Missouri were transferred in 1946.

One special feature surely attracted the New Deal planners to this hilly region as they were thinking about recreation: the lake itself. It was formed in 1931 as the Union Electric Company of St. Louis completed construction of Bagnell Dam on the Osage River, creating the largest hydroelectric impoundment in the Midwest.

The new dam backed water up the meandering main stem of the Osage and its many tributaries, creating a reservoir of 55,342 surface acres with some 1,150 miles of shoreline. Thus it could have lake vistas, swimming beaches, facilities for boating and fish-

Left: Seventeen miles of trails please riders. *Scott Myers* • Right: While some might associate the Lake of the Ozarks with speedboats, there are still plenty of quiet coves for fishing boats and solitude. Two marinas and other boat launch areas give access to 1,150 miles of shoreline, much of which is privately owned. *Nick Decker*

Ozark Caverns in this park is one of four show caves in state parks. You might see a sleeping bat or a blind grotto salamander on a half-mile guided tour.

17,666 acres
Camden and Miller Counties

Trails
- Aquatic Trail (9.75 mi)
- Bluestem Knoll Trail (0.8 mi)
- Coakley Hollow Trail (1 mi)
- Fawn's Ridge Trail (1.25 mi)
- Hidden Springs Trail (2.5 mi)
- Honey Run Trail (12.75 mi)
- Lake Trail (1.5 mi)
- Lakeview Bend Trail (1.5 mi)
- Rocky Top Trail (2 mi)
- Shady Ridge Trail (1 mi)
- Trail of Four Winds (13.5 mi)
- White Oak Trail (1 mi)
- Woodland Trail (3.25 mi)

Historic Structures
- CCC and WPA group camps

ing as well as camping and picnicking, and miles of trails for nature lovers and seekers of solitude. Lake of the Ozarks State Park has all of these within its boundaries. Away from the reservoir, the landscape is largely the dry upland chert woodlands common in this part of the Missouri Ozarks.

Lake of the Ozarks offers excellent opportunities for swimming and boating. Grand Glaize Beach and Public Beach No. 1 are longtime favorites of park users. The park offers a full service, concession-operated marina at Grand Glaize Beach, which also includes one of the larger boat ramps on the lake and provides access to miles of undeveloped shoreline favored by fishermen. A smaller marina at Public Beach No. 1 and other boat launch areas are used by campers and day users. Public access is important, given that most of the lake's shoreline is privately owned.

The lake area is one of the most intensively developed playgrounds in the United States, with many lake roads lined with lodges, restaurants, tackle and curio shops, and a variety of rides, water slides, and other places of entertainment. Indeed, what was once an area catering seasonally to the fishing, boating, swimming, and sunning crowd has now become urbanized with extensive shopping centers and a growing year-round residential population.

It is all the more remarkable that just a short turnoff from the Highway 54 Expressway, one finds the state park, an expansive oasis of natural beauty and tranquility away from the shopping, dining, and many entertainment options. It is the public's great good fortune that the Grand Glaize shores and surrounding lands were kept in the public domain and in their natural state. ∗

Lake Wappapello State Park

Rt 172, Williamsville

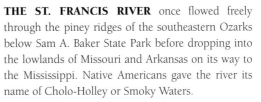

Middle: The fishing is excellent, especially for largemouth bass, crappie, white bass, and bluegill. • Top and bottom: A beach offers swimming and water fun, and you can hike a trail to the Allison family cemetery on the ridge above the lake. Several trails lead into the forest. *All Lauren Stroer*

THE ST. FRANCIS RIVER once flowed freely through the piney ridges of the southeastern Ozarks below Sam A. Baker State Park before dropping into the lowlands of Missouri and Arkansas on its way to the Mississippi. Native Americans gave the river its name of Cholo-Holley or Smoky Waters.

Construction on a dam across the St. Francis River near Wappapello began in 1938 to control flooding along the Mississippi river, and this was the first of the large Army Corps of Engineers dams in Missouri. This was also the site of the first government-funded archaeological survey of a reservoir area in the state.

The park is seldom crowded. Several trails lead along the lake and into the Ozark forest. One arm of the lake is a waterfowl winter refuge, and you can see eagles, ospreys, ducks, and other wildlife. Wappapello is also a convenient point from which to explore corps land that surrounds the lake, the Mark Twain National Forest to the west, nearby Mingo National Wildlife Refuge to the east, and conservation land to the south.

Lake Wappapello is one of the more beautiful corps reservoirs in Missouri. The water is all from the Ozarks, and clear. The hills surrounding the lake are steep and scenic. The forests that cover these slopes are rich and diverse, including species more typical in the Mississippi Lowlands. *

**1,854 acres
Wayne County**

Trails
- Allison Cemetery Trail (2.5 mi)
- Asher Creek Trail (2.75 mi)
- Lakeview (0.7 mi)
- Lake Wappapello Trail (12.75 mi)

Lewis and Clark State Park

801 Lakecrest Blvd, Rushville

The detailed journals that Lewis and Clark left behind show they celebrated the Fourth of July at an oxbow slough they named Gosling Lake on their epic journey up the Missouri River in 1804. *Oliver Schuchard*

JULY 4TH WEDNESDAY [1804] USSERED in the day by a discharge of one shot from our Bow piece, proceeded on, passed the mouth of a Bayeau lading from a large Lake on the S.S. [starboard, or right side] which has the apperance of being once the bed of the river & reaches parrelel for Several Miles.... The before mentioned Lake is clear and Contain great quantities of fish an Gees &. Goslings, The great quantity of those fowl in this Lake induce me to Call it the Gosling Lake.
—William Clark, in *The Journals of the Lewis & Clark Expedition*

In those youthful days of our national independence, it seemed appropriate to Meriwether Lewis and William Clark and their crew to begin the day with a salute from the gun mounted on the bow of their keelboat. That same day, they explored the lake, noted the abundance of goslings on the water, and named it Gosling Lake. Although the shifting of the river's channel makes identification uncertain, Gosling Lake may well be the oxbow known today as Lewis and Clark Lake.

In the summer of 1804, the lower Missouri valley was oppressively hot and uncomfortable. Nevertheless, the journals record a landscape startling to the explorers for its richness and beauty. Enveloping the wide brown river course were rolling hills draped in lush prairies and interspersed with copses of timber. Clark and Lewis comment on the abundant wild game, including deer and turkey, and also on the walnut and "paecaun" (pecan), the wild grapes and raspberries, and the colorful "Parrot queets" (now extinct Carolina parakeets) that wheeled in flocks among the towering riverside trees.

Lewis and Clark State Park, honoring one of the longest expeditions across some of the broadest expanses of the American continent, is less than 200 acres. The lake, at 365 acres, is bigger than the park. Even though it is smaller and probably shallower than it was in 1804, it still provides good catfish fishing.

Just as the oxbow lake at Big Lake State Park does, the oxbow lake here has a tendency to fill in with silt during major floods, such as those in 1993 and 2011. As the lake has filled in, it has become more attractive to waterfowl, and birdwatchers will enjoy seeing the numerous ducks, geese, pelicans, and even swans, especially during migration. The great flood of 1993 led to the closing of the fish hatchery operation here and the ongoing redesign of park facilities to emphasize the Lewis and Clark expedition, the Missouri River, and the evolution of the local landscape.

Though not yet fully operational, the park provides facilities for lakeside picnicking, including a Civilian Conservation Corps-era stone shelter, and a well-appointed campground with friendly little thirteen-lined ground squirrels that scurry around to the delight of campers. A short hiking and biking trail connects the campground with a plaza dedicated in 2004 during the Lewis and Clark bicentennial. The plaza features a walkway suggesting the landscape of the time, complete with meanders, sand bars, and little rolling hills. It overlooks the lake and includes a compass rosette surrounded by stone benches that display the names of members of the Corps of Discovery. You can see a large replica of the keelboat used on the expedition in the park office.

Lewis and Clark State Park commemorates an epic exploration, and it offers a pleasant environment in which to enjoy a remnant landscape of that saga of discovery. *

**189 acres
Buchanan County**

Trail
- Gosling Lake Trail (1.1 mi)

Historic Structure
- CCC shelter

Locust Creek Covered Bridge State Historic Site

16957 Dart Rd, Laclede

BEREFT OF NOT ONLY A ROAD but also a river, one of the four remaining covered bridges in the state sits a few miles west of Gen. John J. Pershing's hometown of Laclede, a reminder of how times have changed in north Missouri. The road leading to the bridge and what was once the channel of Locust Creek were barely visible as faint traces. All had been buried in silt from eroded fields swept down the waterway through the artificially straightened channel.

The bridge is remarkably well preserved, considering it was built in 1868, although much restoration was necessary. This is the longest of the covered bridges surviving in Missouri (all now state historic sites), 151 feet from end to end, 16 feet wide, and 20 feet to the gable. It was built of white pine using the Howe truss method, as were most of the once numerous covered bridges in the state. According to Linn County records, the construction cost was "not to exceed $5,000."

Running parallel to the Hannibal and St. Joseph Railroad, completed before the Civil War, the bridge was situated on what would become the main east-west road across northern Missouri. Built in the days of horses and buggies, the roadway in 1897 accommodated the Buffalo Soldiers Bicycle Corps of the Twenty-fifth Infantry, crossing on their trek from Fort Missoula, Montana, to St. Louis to prove the effectiveness of the bicycle in moving infantry more rapidly than marching. Later, Model Ts, then Model As, rattled across the plank floor in the late 1910s and 1920s, soon outnumbering the horse-drawn wagons and buggies.

As time went on, federal funding had begun to vastly extend the network of good roads, and in 1930, Highway 36 was built one mile to the south. The venerable covered span was about to become a relic.

From the 1920s into the 1950s, stream-straightening fever afflicted north Missouri, including Locust Creek. Silt-laden floodwaters rushing down the "improved" Locust Creek chute piled up north of the tracks, spread over the floodplain, submerged the old road, crept up the side of the old bridge, and dropped the topsoil carried from eroded farmlands up north. The silt buildup was so dramatic that one could scarcely imagine the earthen ramps that were once necessary to provide access to the bridge.

The Linn County government stopped maintaining the road to the bridge in 1960, and the bridge was deeded to the state for preservation as a historic site in 1968, one hundred years after its completion.

A new approach route from the west was completed and dedicated in 1989. Then in 1991, the park division raised the structure three feet, rebuilt the abutments, and constructed new approaches, so that the bridge would again look more like a bridge and also to lift the bottom of the bridge chords off the ground, where they would be less exposed to flooding and soil moisture.

At one time, there was talk of moving the abandoned and isolated bridge to Pershing State Park several miles to the south. But here is where memories were made at square dances, at weddings held in it, and at picnics enjoyed nearby. Here the bridge remains. ✳

Left: The bridge was constructed using a Howe Truss, once the gold standard in bridge building. *Missouri State Parks* • Right: Pershing State Park now surrounds the high and dry historic site, home of the longest remaining covered bridge in Missouri. *Kyle Spradley*

A large red and white sign with the bold black letters PP-OO was likely once nailed to the bridge, as the Pikes Peak Ocean to Ocean Highway crossed here. The PP-OO Association promoted its route as "The Appian Way of America, the military commercial main-line across the United States."

32 acres
Linn County

Construction of the Long Branch Dam came none too soon to save remnants of northern Missouri's tallgrass prairie and oak savanna. With the Bee Trace area in the park, prescribed fires and removal of scrub brush from pastures and woodlots have restored its health and species diversity, making it northeastern Missouri's most important prairie and savanna.

**1,829 acres
Macon County**

Trails
- Bee Trace Trail (7.5 mi)
- Lakeview Trail (0.6 mi)
- Little Chariton Prairie Trail (1.5 mi)

Long Branch State Park

28615 Visitor Center Rd, Macon

PIONEERS FROM THE APPALACHIAN hills and valleys of North Carolina and Kentucky followed Daniel Boone into Missouri in the early 1800s, and some of them continued on into the area north of the Missouri River. Traveling westward along the Salt River, a Mississippi River tributary, or northward from the Missouri River via the Chariton River, they converged on an ancient American Indian trade route that followed high ground marking the geographical divide between the Mississippi and Missouri drainages, known as the Grand Divide. Thus, they found the land that is now Randolph, Macon, and Adair counties, and it reminded them of home.

In 1965, Congress authorized a dam, a multipurpose project for flood control, water supply, and recreation for the area. The 2,430-acre reservoir it formed is Long Branch Lake, and the park surrounds the lower reaches of the reservoir.

Some 640 acres of the Bee Trace area, where settlers harvested honey, lie within the park. Here, great white oaks that were saplings when the first settlers came in search of honey loom over an open understory of prairie grasses, sedges, and wildflowers. Core drillings have revealed one tree that has stood for more than 250 years. It was the white and bur oaks—given their tendency to have hollow trunks and limbs—that provided homes for the wild honeybee.

Long Branch State Park also reveals evidence of occupation by American Indians. Just as the environment of northern Missouri was highly structured with narrow fingers of woodland extending along the streams, with the broad sweep of prairie beyond, so too were the locations of American Indian sites. From about 9,000 to 1,500 years ago, most sites were occupied seasonally in late summer and fall for large-scale processing of nuts, as indicated by the unusually high concentrations of nutting stones in proportion to projectile points.

Long Branch Lake with its sparkling blue water satisfies an ancestral hunger for a good fishing hole. It has become famous for crappie and catfish. It is also popular for boating, waterskiing, and swimming. Here, you can appreciate the environment that is and was north Missouri. *

Top: Families enjoy the sand beach at the park. *Ben Nickelson* Middle: The West Chariton Prairie unit of the Chariton River Hills Natural Area at Long Branch offers a glimpse of the prairie landscape of native grasses and wildflowers that once covered much of northern and western Missouri. *Scott Myers* • Rattlesnake master blooms among 200-year-old white oaks on this remnant of north Missouri savanna in the Bee Trace area. Honeybees and bats favored hollow trees in these open woodlands and prairies. *Ken McCarty*

Mark Twain Birthplace State Historic Site

37352 Shrine Rd, Florida

IN A RENTED TWO-ROOM clapboard cabin, Samuel Langhorne Clemens was born on November 30, 1835. He was the sixth child of John and Jane Clemens. That cabin still stands, protected by a museum.

Merritt Alexander "Dad" Violette, whose mother had known the Clemens family in Florida, Missouri, bought the deteriorated cabin in 1915 and moved it across the street to property he owned. Later, with his backing, the Mark Twain Memorial Park Association was organized and bought land adjacent to Florida for a park to memorialize Twain. Violette presented the cabin to the association, and then it transferred the cabin and land to the state. This was the first state park north of the Missouri River.

The cabin was moved in 1930 from Florida to the new park, where it was placed on the highest point of old Hilltop Camp, a girls camp Violette had run. A primitive frame shelter protected it somewhat from the weather. In 1960, an ultra-modern museum building, complete with a hyperbolic paraboloid roof, was dedicated, and the simple two-room cabin now sits inside. The contrast between the soaring roof and the little cabin on the red tile floor is striking.

The museum contains a wealth of artifacts, exhibits, books, and a public reading room An original handwritten manuscript of *The Adventures of Tom Sawyer* and a galley proof with his handwritten notes and corrections are on view. *

Upon seeing a picture of the simple cabin he was born in years after having moved, Mark Twain wrote, "Heretofore, I have always stated that it was a palace, but I shall be more guarded now."

**13 acres
Monroe County**

Top: The Clemens family moved out of the cabin to Hannibal in 1839, just a few years after Samuel Clemens was born, but he returned to an uncle's farm nearby to spend many summers. Bottom: The Mark Twain Shrine was dedicated in 1960 and was the first modern visitor center and museum in a Missouri park. It now protects the cabin from the elements. *Both Oliver Schuchard*

Mark Twain State Park

37352 Shrine Rd, Florida

Buzzard's Roost once looked across the Salt River valley Sam Clemens loved to roam as a boy. Today, it still attracts people to spectacular views of Mark Twain Lake. *Missouri State Parks*

AFTER THE MARK TWAIN MEMORIAL PARK Association formally dedicated its new park in honor of Monroe County's native son in August 1924, it transferred the land to the state. Mark Twain State Park was one of the first parks in the state's new park system and, for years, the only one north of the Missouri River. Some of the hundred-acre park was formerly a girls' camp operated by M. A. "Dad" Violette of Florida, one of the founders of the park association. The park eventually provided a hilltop setting for the relocated birthplace cabin of Mark Twain, which Violette had saved from destruction. Mark Twain was born as Samuel Clemens in 1835 in the tiny settlement of Florida, its remains now surrounded by the park and, since 1983, by the huge Mark Twain Lake.

Much of the early development at the park occurred between 1939 and 1942, when Civilian Conservation Corps (CCC) Company 1743, an all-black company that had done superb work at Washington State Park, was transferred here. Some local residents, forgetting the lessons of Huck and Jim, circulated petitions protesting the assignment of black workers to the park, but other citizens, who did remember, circulated counter-petitions and carried the day. The CCC cleared large tracts of land, laid out trails, installed a water system, and developed a beautiful picnic area amid generous shade trees at Buzzard's Roost, a promontory overlooking the Salt River valley, which is today Mark Twain Lake. The picnic ground features a T-shaped, open shelter, built of native limestone, with a large stone fireplace flanked by built-in stone benches with wood seats.

For decades, Mark Twain State Park consisted of rugged, timbered hills surrounding and overlooking the north and middle forks of the scenic Salt River. In these valleys and along these streams, Missourians were invited to play and explore, just as a young Sam Clemens had done.

But in 1983, the Army Corps of Engineers completed Clarence Cannon Dam on the Salt River, creating the 18,000-acre Mark Twain Lake and totally changing the character of the park. Enlarged to 2,775 acres by the addition of land leased from the corps, the park is now reservoir-based and provides facilities geared toward water recreation, including boat ramps and a beach. The most attractive picnicking spot in the park, however, is still the old Buzzard's Roost. Camp Clemens has been closed, and a modern group camp was constructed on land acquired from the corps. The camp is named Camp Colborn, after R. I. "Si" Colborn, the longtime editor of the *Monroe County Appeal* and a Missouri State Park Board member during the 1950s and 1960s, as well as the leader of the counter-petition effort back in 1939 to bring the black CCC company to the park.

Away from the developments, there is still a large area of fairly wild land. Because of the deep valleys carved by the Salt River and its tributaries, the park has an Ozark-like quality in contrast to most of the rolling glaciated plains of agricultural north Missouri. The extent of the park's woodlands of oak, hickory, and maple, coupled with those owned by the corps around virtually the entire lake, make this area one of the most significant examples of a north-central Missouri forested landscape.

Beyond the reservoir and its wooded fringe, the lovely rolling fields and farms and the friendly people of Monroe County are still there, and the country still offers the perfect setting for a lazy summer of fishing, swimming, and dreaming. *

2,775 acres
Monroe County

Trails
- Barefoot Sam Trail (0.4 mi)
- Dogwood Trail (2.25 mi)
- Post Oak Trail (1.75 mi)
- White Oak Trail (1.25 mi)
- Whitetail Trail (0.5 mi)

Historic Structure
- Buzzard's Roost picnic area and other CCC structures

Mastodon State Historic Site

1050 Charles J Becker Dr, Imperial

THE KIMMSWICK BONE BEDS at this site are where scientists discovered the first solid evidence of the coexistence of humans and the American mastodon in North America. The initial 418 acres of Mastodon State Park were acquired in 1966 by the State Highway Department as part of the right-of-way for Interstate 55 heading south out of St. Louis. Four years later, after completing the new highway, the department declared the acreage surplus property and planned to auction it off. Local residents, long proud of the historic significance of self-styled naturalist Albert C. Koch's discovery of the bone beds and of the scenic beauty of the area, worked to create a park.

But a state archaeological survey presented to the State Park Board a month later dashed cold water on their dreams. The report expressed doubts concerning the extent of undisturbed Pleistocene deposits remaining. To try to put to rest the putative connection of mastodon bones with human artifacts, the survey report stated, "No cultural material has ever been found at the site to show man's involvement and contemporaneity with these mastodons."

Fortunately, four area women did not listen to all the expert advice they were receiving but organized the Mastodon Park Committee and got to work. Their ceaseless lobbying of local representatives and other efforts were acknowledged in 1975 when the legislature appropriated $200,000 in state funds toward the purchase. By a deadline that had been set, they had raised enough additional money on their own.

Almost immediately after beginning digging at in May 1979, Illinois researchers discovered a Clovis point, an ancient, distinctively shaped projectile, in direct association with mastodon bones. The discovery here is the first undisputed evidence of of humans and mastodons together in North America. Bones from a giant ground sloth, a giant armadillo, a bison, a miniature horse, a wild pig, a stag moose, and some other extinct species have also been found.

A visitors center leads you back through the epochs of human and natural history in the area. Children can touch a mastodon tooth, and a replica of a giant ground sloth enthralls everyone. An exit to a trail that winds past the Charles Callison Memorial Bird Sanctuary and down the hill leads you to the excavation site at the base. *

Top: A full-size replica of a mastodon skeleton looms over an exhibit and shows the scale of the creatures. *Missouri Department of Natural Resources* • Middle: Archaeologists have now preserved the dig site for the future. • Bottom: A volunteer helps visitors investigate fossils during a special event. *Both Missouri State Parks*

Mastodon State Park was very nearly sold to St. Louis developers, but the efforts of locals Dorothy Heinze, Marilyn King, Hazel Lee, and Rita Naes, who called themselves the Mastodon Park Committee, coupled with their belief that the site had something significant buried beneath its surface, saved the area and gave us the park.

**431 acres
Jefferson County**

Trails
- Limestone Hill Trail (2 mi)
- Spring Branch Trail (0.8 mi)
- Wildflower Trail (0.4 mi)

Meramec State Park

115 Meramec Park Dr, Sullivan

ONE OF FIVE STATE PARKS along the Meramec River, Meramec State Park is one of the oldest, best known, and most popular of Missouri's state parks. This park is one of the largest in the state, lying across parts of three counties. It has some four dozen named caves within its boundaries, more than any other state park in Missouri and second in the nation.

The park traces its beginnings to 1927, when the State Game and Fish Commission started acquiring land along the river near the site of the old mining town, Reedsville. Indians and early French and American settlers had mined there for lead, and later also for iron and copper. With easy accessibility from St. Louis, some ten thousand people in two thousand cars reportedly attended the park dedication in 1928.

The Civilian Conservation Corps (CCC) built many of the facilities in the 1930s. Most of these structures, including the dining lodge, cabins, and river shelter, have been restored and are still in service. The vintage lodge offers a fine view of the river. Newer facilities such as the park store, Hickory Ridge Conference Center, and visitor center were designed to carry on the CCC heritage of craftsmanship.

Near the riverside campground is the entrance to Fisher Cave, one of Missouri's oldest show caves. The cave features many speleothems (rock forms) with troglobites and stygobites (cave creatures). Fisher Cave was key in the 1950s studies of prominent geologist J. Harlan Bretz when he was developing his

Left: Bleeding shiners, found in the cool, clear Meramec, display breeding colors. *William Roston* • Right: The Meramec River flows more than eight miles through and alongside the park. *Ron Colatskie*

The Meramec River narrowly avoided becoming a dammed-up lake after strong public opinion and a regional vote persuaded lawmakers to abandon the project.

6,896 acres Crawford, Franklin, and Washington Counties

Trails
- Bluff View Trail (1.5 mi)
- Deer Hollow Trail (1.25 mi)
- Hamilton Iron Works Trail (0.2 mi)
- Natural Wonders Trail (1.25 mi)
- River Trail (0.75 mi)
- Walking Fern Trail (0.5 mi)
- Wilderness Trail (8.5 mi)

Historic Structures
- CCC dining lodge, cabins, and river shelter

theory of speleogenesis, or cave origin.

Wildlife abounds in the park, and you will have a good chance of seeing ospreys, mink, or river otters. September is often the best month to be on the river. Typically, skies are sunny, temperatures are mild, and the river is clear and uncrowded. In mid-September, the peak of the hummingbird migration usually coincides with the peak blooming of the cardinal flower, which attracts the birds in droves.

Even at midday on a summer weekend, you can experience the rich diversity of the Meramec by putting on snorkeling goggles and submerging into the clear waters. With over one hundred species of fish and numerous species of turtles, salamanders, crawfish, and mussels, the Meramec is considered Missouri's Amazon of aquatic life.

Some of the best places to experience the harmonious blend of glades and majestic trees are the park's two natural areas, the 460-acre Meramec Upland Forest Natural Area and the 830-acre Meramec Mosaic Natural Area. They represent some of Missouri's finest examples of the forest and woodland communities that typically grow on well-drained cherty soil formed from dolomite rock. The Mosaic area may be entered on the mile-long Natural Wonders Trail near the visitor center while the ten-mile Wilderness Trail traverses the remote Upland Forest area and adjacent backcountry in the northern part of the park.

Although the woods and the caves provide an extra measure of enjoyment for a Meramec State Park outing, it is ultimately the natural values of the river and its rugged watershed that define not only the experience but also the park itself. *

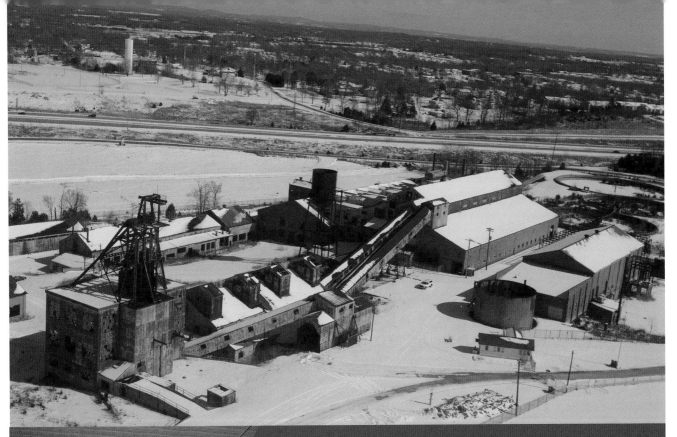

Missouri Mines
State Historic Site

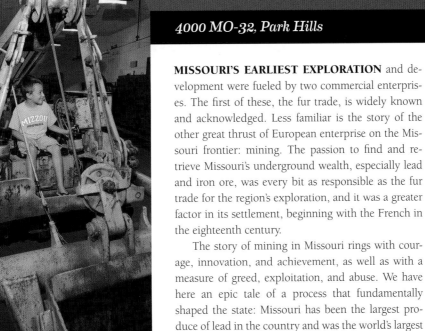

MISSOURI'S EARLIEST EXPLORATION and development were fueled by two commercial enterprises. The first of these, the fur trade, is widely known and acknowledged. Less familiar is the story of the other great thrust of European enterprise on the Missouri frontier: mining. The passion to find and retrieve Missouri's underground wealth, especially lead and iron ore, was every bit as responsible as the fur trade for the region's exploration, and it was a greater factor in its settlement, beginning with the French in the eighteenth century.

The story of mining in Missouri rings with courage, innovation, and achievement, as well as with a measure of greed, exploitation, and abuse. We have here an epic tale of a process that fundamentally shaped the state: Missouri has been the largest produce of lead in the country and was the world's largest lead producer for a time. This important story needs to be told, and Missouri Mines State Historic Site is dedicated to that mission.

The museum includes an extraordinary physical plant and mineral collections. Mining has been from the beginning an integral part of the state's heritage. Missouri Mines State Historic Site tells the exciting story of that epic saga, amid the hulking structures and machinery that were a part of it. *

In 1975, the St. Joe Minerals Corporation offered the entire Federal Mill complex to Missouri, forming the basis for the site that exists today. It preserves 25 mining structures, including the large powerhouse, which now serves as a mining equipment, history, and mineral museum.

**65 acres
St. Francois
County**

Top: The maze of buildings and other structures at Federal Mill No. 3 comprises one of the most extraordinary mining museums in the United States. It's located in the Old Lead Belt, a legendary mining region in the United States. *Ron Colatskie* • Bottom: The Powerhouse Museum displays massive equipment such as this St. Joe shovel. The mechanical loader on tracks is unique, designed specifically for Old Lead Belt conditions. Fifty-two were built here. *Missouri State Parks*

Missouri State Museum

at the Capitol, near Jefferson Landing State Historic Site

201 W Capitol Ave, Jefferson City

FIRST-TIME VISITORS to the state Capitol may be surprised to discover that their guides wear state park uniforms. In 1976 responsibility for the Missouri State Museum and educational efforts about the capitol and its extraordinary public art were vested in the park division, thanks largely to its successful development of the adjacent Jefferson Landing State Historic Site.

A museum was planned for the Capitol from the start. The architects designed a 60-by-112-foot-long museum gallery on each side of the rotunda. On the ground floor, the galleries extend two stories high, with a mezzanine at the second-floor level. Shortly after construction, the Missouri General Assembly defined the themes of the museum galleries. First came the historical museum in the east wing, designated in an act of 1919 as the Missouri Soldiers and Sailors Memorial Hall. Then in 1921, the assembly created the Resources Museum in the west wing to display "the products of the mines, mills, fields, and forests of this state."

The two museums were combined in 1923 and designated collectively as the Missouri State Museum. The museum continued to grow and change over the next five decades, for a time in the 1930s even being called The People's University. Its administration ranged through several state agencies before its 1976 transfer to State Parks. The park division then planned and oversaw a million-dollar renovation of the museum, its first major updating in nearly fifty years, with a special appropriation secured through the efforts of spouses of legislators.

Visitors can learn Missouri's history from both long-term and temporary exhibits. Most of the exhibits, which change regularly to highlight different topics, themes, and eras, include interactive elements as well as artifacts from the museum's vast collections. The museum also presents the state's heritage in educational programming, workshops, and special events of all kinds.

In the Resources Museum, exhibits are arranged according to the six natural divisions of the state, with ingenious cutaway dioramas portraying the characteristic landforms and landscapes of each. The Foundations gallery under the governor's stairs in the rotunda focuses on the previous Capitols in Jefferson City and on Missouri state government. As in the other galleries, the artifacts rotate over time to bring out different pieces from the museum's collections, such as legisla-

Long-term and temporary exhibits, a Missouri Veterans Gallery, displays about the state's natural resources, and superb artwork give visitors a thorough overview of Missouri history. *Missouri State Parks*

tive desks from the Capitol destroyed in the 1911 fire.

Missouri boasts a truly distinguished state Capitol, one that reflects the best of Missouri's people and government. Its setting could hardly be better: in the heartland of the state on a bluff overlooking the broad and fertile valley of the Missouri River, a historic transportation corridor that was a key to the state's development, and backed by a city large enough to provide many urban amenities yet small enough to retain the flavor of rural Missouri.

The building is literally a museum of public art, remarkable both for its quality and abundance and for faithfully reflecting the state as well as its people. Tours of the Capitol cover all major aspects of the building, its artwork, and the Missouri State Museum on the first floor.

The Missouri State Museum and the magnificent Capitol that houses it represent a triumph of vision and vigilance by Missourians who dared to believe that their state could accomplish something truly great. ∗

Thomas Hart Benton's mural, **The Social History of the State of Missouri***, commissioned in 1935, covers all four walls of the house lounge in the Capitol.*

Cole County

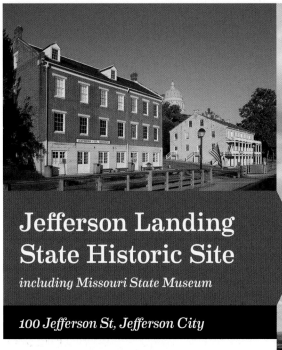

Jefferson Landing State Historic Site

including Missouri State Museum

100 Jefferson St, Jefferson City

WHEN CAPT. CHARLES B. MAUS returned home to Jefferson City in 1865 after Civil War service in the federal army, he changed the name of the hotel he had built in the 1850s to more forcefully demonstrate his wartime sentiments. That's how the old Veranda Hotel at the base of Jefferson Street on the Missouri River landing became the Union Hotel.

The lower end of Jefferson Street had been a lively commercial and transportation hub ever since the state's seat of government moved to Jefferson City from St. Charles. In 1839 James A. Crump built a sturdy three-unit row building of locally quarried stone that served as grocery store, warehouse, tavern, telegraph office, and hotel for the growing state capital traffic. In 1852, Charles F. Lohman bought a portion of the stone building now known as the Lohman building. Three years later, Charles Maus built his own new brick hotel and warehouse building across Jefferson Street from the stone building.

After the war and Charles Maus's rechristening of the Union Hotel, Missouri River traffic began a steady decline. Maus and Lohman's son Louis later relocated their commercial activity to Jefferson City's High Street in the mid-1870s. The old hotel, warehouse, and store buildings were almost torn down in the late 1960s. But an alert local citizenry, led by Elizabeth Rozier, gained a reprieve for this river-front complex. Four years later, state park officials proposed to restore the buildings to correct period appearance and open them to the public. All three of the remaining historic structures at the landing—the Lohman building, the Union Hotel, and the Christopher Maus home—were restored in time for their dedication on July 4, 1976.

Jefferson Landing tells the story of how Missouri grew during the mid-nineteenth century. Freight shipped to or from Jefferson City or transferred there from rail to steamboat was warehoused in these build-

Top left: The red brick Union hotel and the stone Lohman building are part of Missouri's oldest intact river landing. *Missouri State Parks* • Above: This view of the landing is from the Capitol dome. *Scott Myers*

ings while awaiting the next leg of a western journey.

The ground floor of the stone Lohman building houses an exhibit area that tells the story of Jefferson City and the landing through exhibits, designed to appear as a mid-nineteenth-century general store and warehouse. The second floor of the Union Hotel houses an art and history gallery. The bottom level of the hotel has been restored to something of its old-time bustle through its use as the Amtrak train station.

Originally, all lines of communication crossed at the landing—steamboat, river ferry, stagecoach, telegraph, and railroad. The hotels, saloons, warehouses, and mercantile establishments provided business activity by day and social activity by night. Today, the landing is once again a gathering place for special events indoors and on the grounds. *

Missouri was the main conduit of westward expansion—much of that migration went through Jefferson Landing.

1 acre
Cole County

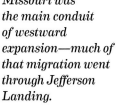

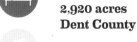

Montauk Spring today really consists of multiple springs, but back before the turn of the twentieth century, there was a single big spring outlet. Legend says someone proved that spring was at least 250 feet deep. In 1892, a downpour washed sand, gravel, and debris into the spring.

2,920 acres
Dent County

Trails
- Montauk Lake Trail (0.8 mi)
- Paved Bicycle Trail (0.1 mi)
- Pine Ridge Trail (1.5 mi)

Historic Structures
- Gristmill dating to 1896
- CCC-built dam, shelters, and cabins

Montauk State Park

345 County Rd 6670, Salem

A SERIES OF SPRINGS adjacent to Pigeon Creek provide the origin of the Current River, which begins its journey south in Montauk State Park. More than forty million gallons of cool, clear water bubble up daily from the ancient dolomites lying under this park. Leonard Hall, the dean of Missouri's conservation writers, put it best: "One thing which makes Current River unique is that it lives out its entire life within the heart of the Ozark highland and thus is always in character."

One of the first-generation of parks, acquired by the state in 1926, Montauk is perhaps best known as one of Missouri's four trout parks. The secluded setting has over three miles of fishing stream and woodlands, which give Montauk a more primitive feel than the state's other trout parks. The long, cold spring branches of Montauk provide an ideal habitat for hatchery-bred rainbow trout.

Almost any weekend from early spring to late fall, anglers from Missouri and other states flock to the park and line up along the "runs," trying to catch one of the delectable beauties released to the wild every day. The most extraordinary spectacle is the old-fashioned trout opening-day ritual on March 1 each year. Thousands of ardent anglers descend on the park the day before, and some stay up all night visiting with friends and readying equipment, the better to jockey for position in the cold dawn as they wait for the opening siren.

Rising from the springs and hatchery area, steep wooded ridges hem in the fledgling Current River, forming a narrow valley of superb, scenic beauty. The slopes are covered with a mature woodland of white oak, shortleaf pine, black oak, northern red oak, and maple. In places, the river flows below tall pine-capped bluffs of stained dolomite. The park is well-known for its spring wildflower display—the fire pinks, blue phlox, and many more.

Montauk State Park offers a variety of accommodations: campgrounds, housekeeping cabins, a motel, and the Dorman L. Steelman Lodge. During the winter months, catch-and-release angling is available. During the regular fishing season, there are trout derbies and mill tours, hikes, and amphitheater programs led by interpreters. Opening day or any day, Montauk State Park is a treasure. ✳

Top: A cold morning's mist surrounds an ardent fisherman. *Scott Myers* • Middle: A pair of eagles built their nest on a ridge-top pine in 2000 and have been successfully raising young here ever since. *Larry Sportman* • Bottom: Kids of all ages love to fish for trout here, even during the cold catch-and-release season. *Steve Bost*

Morris State Park

Hwy WW, Campbell

This area was used extensively by Native Americans and then settled in 1821 by Benjamin Crowley, which is how Crowley's Ridge got its name.

161 acres
Dunklin County

Trail
• Beech Tree Trail (2.25 mi)

IT'S A SMALL PARK, BUT IT HAS A BIG geologic story to tell. It nestles on the east flank of Crowley's Ridge amongst surrounding peach orchards and is nearly all wooded. Here in the heart of the continent, Gulf of Mexico waters once formed a huge bay that geologists call the Mississippi Embayment. How this bay formed, filled in, eroded out, and left behind a bedrock, gravel, and soil spine several hundred feet high and some 150 miles long down its middle is a complex geological story. That spine is Crowley's Ridge. As a resource-preservation park, the main offering is a two-mile ramble on Beech Tree Trail.

The loop trail provides an accessible scenic overlook of the surrounding alluvial plain, but it is quite steep in places as it descends to the bottomland forest and then back up. In several spots, the sequential geologic strata that built the ridge are well displayed—or at least those of the last few hundred thousand years.

There is a final surprise—a complement of trees and plants restricted to this region of Missouri. The woods of Morris State Park more resemble the forests of the Appalachian Mountains than they do the Ozarks. The entire park is mature sand woodland, a rare natural community in Missouri. The park has more than 325 species of plants, and the flora of ten thousand years ago still persists. ∗

Top: American beech trees typical of the Appalachians grow in the woodlands here. *Allison Vaughn* • Bottom: Crowley's Ridge extends for about 150 miles through the Mississippi Lowlands of Missouri and Arkansas. It was carved by the ancestral Mississippi River flowing to its west and the Ohio River to its east. *Wikipedian Kbh3rd*

Jay Nixon State Park

Rt N southwest of Ironton

MOUNTAINTOP LAKES ARE RARE in Missouri, and this park in the St. Francois Mountains has this feature not previously found in any Missouri state park.

The new park is at the northwest corner of Taum Sauk Mountain State Park and is bordered by the Ketcherside Mountain Conservation Area.

At present, the only access to the park is from the Ozark Trail, which runs some 390 miles from St. Louis to the Arkansas border and links Taum Sauk and Johnson's Shut-Ins State Parks. Plans have not been finalized for trails that would allow hikers and campers access to the park.

The lake was formed by a sturdy rock-and-earthen dam that was believed to have been constructed in the 1970s. The dam impounded waters that flow from two spring branches that emerge from the forested hillside.

The lake presents a unique recreational opportunity not available before in the state park system. It has the potential for fishing, boating, and camping. The lake is about 30 feet deep and home to a bountiful supply of bluegill and largemouth bass. The surrounding land is heavily wooded, with rocky glades in the occasional break in the forest. At one end of the dam, the overflow from the lake forms a small waterfall as it tumbles down the spillway of bedrock. ✳

The park is named for former Gov. Jay Nixon, who made improving and expanding the state park system a priority. During his two terms, years of declining attendance were reversed, and in 2016, a record of more than 20 million people visited state parks.

1,230 acres
Reynolds County

Top: The 64-acre clear, cold mountaintop lake is the size of 50 football fields, perfect for fishing. Above: A waterfall tumbles over the spillway of the dam that formed the lake. *Both Tom Uhlenbrock*

Onondaga Cave State Park

7556 Rt H, Leasburg

THE CROWN JEWEL in Missouri's underground treasure chest is Onondaga Cave. Meramec State Park, just twenty miles downstream, has the greatest number of caves, but Onondaga Cave State Park has the preeminent cave. For more than seventy-five years before its 1982 acquisition as a park, Onondaga Cave was one of the major public attractions in the Midwest, and it still is.

More than thirty known caves are in the park, more than any other park except Meramec. Two are well-known, Onondaga and Cathedral, and both had long histories as show caves. A naming contest in conjunction with the World's Fair in 1904 settled one cave's name as Onondaga, which is the name of a tribe of the Iroquois and means "spirit of the hills.'

In 1949, Onondaga Cave began its ascent to national notoriety when it was sold to Lyman Riley and Lester B. Dill. Under their leadership, Onondaga reached its commercial apogee in the 1950s and 1960s as a nationally known show cave. Dill became sole owner in the late 1960s, and his remarkable personality has left its indelible mark on Onondaga Cave and Missouri's tourism industry. Dill had an Ozark wit and a legendary gift for telling tall tales. He always told what he called the Ozark truth—something between the honest truth and a bald-faced lie—like the time he promoted a 102-year-old Oklahoman named J. Frank Dalton as the real, still-living Jesse James. He became known as "America's Number One Caveman," but he always called himself a "caveologist." His stubborn resistance to the Army Corps of Engineers helped save the cave and much of the surrounding Meramec River valley from permanent flooding by the proposed Meramec Dam.

In 1980, Onondaga Cave won designation by the National Park Service as a National Natural Landmark, a testament to its value to science and to Dill's respect for the natural integrity of the cave. Before his death, Dill had already begun talks on turning Onondaga Cave into a state park. With the cooperation of the Dill estate, his desire to preserve Onondaga for future generations was realized with the dedication of the state park—and presentation of the national landmark plaque—in 1982.

Park staff recently discovered yet another passage in Onondaga, which added 310 feet to the known cave. The new addition contains remains of several ice age animals, further contributions of the cave to scientific discovery. Park naturalists and interpreters lead cave tours.

There are attractions outside, too. Vilander Bluff is the tallest bluff on the Meramec River. Its projecting overhangs loom above canoeists below. Hike along the trail and see ancient eastern red cedars. Seventy of them are over three hundred years old, and some are up to five hundred years. Dislodged skeletons of these ancient trees lie scattered at the base of the cliff. The Vilander Bluff Natural Area includes a trail leading you through bottomland forest, the bluff, the caves, and an upland chert woodland and savanna.

Saved from fate as a mine by becoming a major attraction at a world's fair and then surviving as a show cave with creative marketing, Onondaga Cave and the park continue to awe park visitors today. *

Left: Views of the Meramec River from the Vilander Bluff Natural Area are as spectacular as the splendid formations that await inside Onondaga Cave. *Missouri State Parks* • Right: Stone lily pads in the cave have formed drop by drop over eons. *Scott Myers*

George Bothe, who owned the cave in 1904, arranged for visitors at the World's Fair to come and see the cave by way of the Frisco Railroad, in which he was an investor. Thousands of visitors made the journey out to view the cave.

1,358 acres
Crawford County

Trails
- Amphitheater Trail (0.6 mi
- Blue Heron Trail (0.5 mi)
- Deer Run Trail (2.25 mi)
- Oak Ridge Trail (3 mi)
- Vilander Bluff Trail (1.25 mi)

Osage Village State Historic Site

Hwy C, Walker

The Osage had their main village on a grass-covered hilltop in this mostly open landscape. From their village, the Osage dominated a wide swath of prairies and woodlands. *Missouri State Parks*

THE TRIBE MOST FEARED and respected by other natives when French-speaking explorers and traders first came to Missouri called themselves the Ni-U-Ko'n-Ska, "Children of the Middle Waters." Among themselves, in humility before their Wah'Kon, or "Mystery Force," they said they were the "Little Ones." The first written record of this tribe derives from the expedition of Louis Jolliet and Father Jacques Marquette down the Mississippi River in 1673. Their principal villages were at a junction of waters in western Missouri that they called the Place-of-Many-Swans. The Osage were lords of the prairies and woodlands from the Missouri River to the Arkansas River, and from the Mississippi River to the Great Plains. It is startling to consider that this robust, warlike tribe numbering at most ten thousand people so thoroughly dominated such a large region. The land, which they called "The Sacred One," was certainly rich, and the Osage obviously knew how to live on it.

The arrival of the earliest French traders from the east and of the first stray horses from the southwest probably did not affect the Osage as drastically as the tribes farther west on the plains. Neither the French, the Spanish, nor the British could contest the power of the Osage in their domain. Instead, the Osage were prime trading partners, supplying huge quantities of furs and also captive Indian slaves.

When the young United States bought the territory of Louisiana from France in 1803, the old Osage way of life was doomed. American settlers pressed hard upon Osage lands. Starting with a treaty in 1808, the Osage withdrew step-by-painful-step from Missouri and eventually into Oklahoma, where they now live. The Osage domain today is but one oil-rich county in Oklahoma: Osage County.

During the period from about 1700, not long after they first met the French traders, until about 1775, when they moved a few miles away to the south, the lodges of the Little Ones stood on a high, open hilltop that commands a sweeping view of the winding Osage River valley and surrounding hills and groves. This hill is the highest in a chain of isolated, limestone-capped remnant hills that runs roughly northwest to southeast, sitting between two small tributary streams and pointing toward the Osage River to the north. It is this grass-covered hilltop site that is now preserved as Osage Village State Historic Site.

In 1941, a young archaeologist from the University of Missouri surveyed the site and confirmed that this hill was indeed a principal village site of the Osage during those historic decades of the eighteenth century. The extent of the site was more precisely defined through excavations over the years, and a wealth of recovered artifacts now documents the village. Evidence suggests that at its height the village had two to three thousand inhabitants living in about two hundred lodges.

In its lovely setting with its wealth of buried knowledge and because of its pivotal role in so much early Missouri history, Osage Village State Historic Site has a unique part to play in helping Missourians understand their state. Though the site has been left undeveloped in an effort to preserve what remains, the one-mile walking trail with excellent outdoor exhibits helps the visitor not only to visualize the history of the Osage and the relationship of this place to other nearby Osage and early European sites but also to sense something of what life must have been like in this vibrant Native American village. *

**100 Acres
Vernon County**

Trail
• Interpretive Trail (0.8 mi)

Ozark Mountain State Park

Northwest of Branson

SPECTACULAR VIEWS of the surrounding wooded hills and valleys will be available from this park, as the four mountains here rise four hundred feet above the surrounding land. The prominent feature on the horizon is the Shepherd of the Hills Inspiration Tower, a landmark on the Branson entertainment strip.

The ridges and hills have only scattered trees at the top, and are known locally as knobs. They gave the name "baldknobbers" to hooded vigilante groups that legend says met on the barren hilltops.

The knobs and their glades are home to specialized plants and animals that thrive in the rocky, sun-drenched conditions. The result is an open, grassy, flower-filled landscape of hilltops rising above the forest, hollows, and river valley.

Ozark Mountain State Park includes 2.2 miles of Roark Creek, a clear stream with white slab bedrock. The land abuts the Henning Conservation Area, which is on the west end of Branson's Country Music Boulevard and offers a popular respite for hikers and birders.

The park includes a unique one-room schoolhouse that served the long-gone community of Garber. It also contains old roads, potential trails that could connect to those in the conservation area. ∗

A hike to the top of the knobs will be a breathtaking experience, literally, and offer breathtaking views.

**1,011 Acres
Taney County**

Historic Structure
• A one-room schoolhouse with two front doors

Top: The treeless knobs here contain rocky glades that are home to specialized plants and animals. Bottom: Roark Creek runs for 2.2 miles through the park. *Both Tom Uhlenbrock*

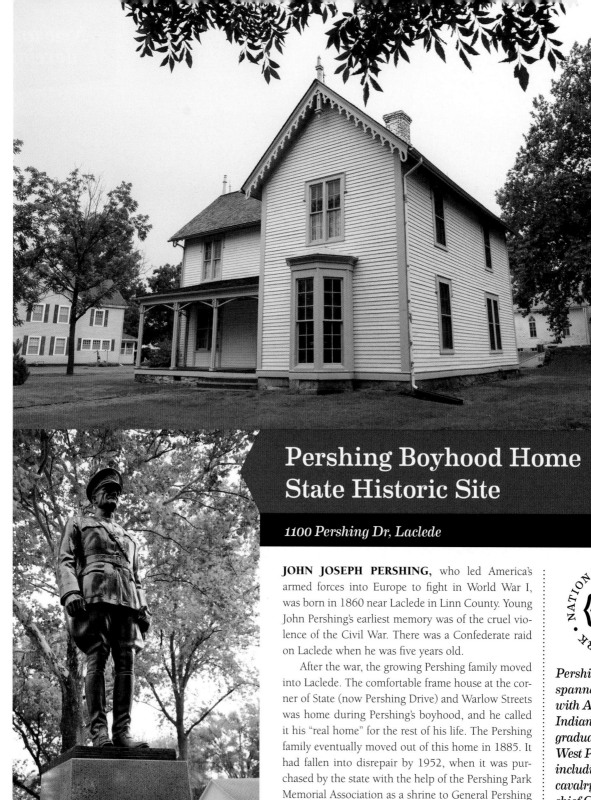

Pershing Boyhood Home State Historic Site

1100 Pershing Dr, Laclede

JOHN JOSEPH PERSHING, who led America's armed forces into Europe to fight in World War I, was born in 1860 near Laclede in Linn County. Young John Pershing's earliest memory was of the cruel violence of the Civil War. There was a Confederate raid on Laclede when he was five years old.

After the war, the growing Pershing family moved into Laclede. The comfortable frame house at the corner of State (now Pershing Drive) and Warlow Streets was home during Pershing's boyhood, and he called it his "real home" for the rest of his life. The Pershing family eventually moved out of this home in 1885. It had fallen into disrepair by 1952, when it was purchased by the state with the help of the Pershing Park Memorial Association as a shrine to General Pershing and the American soldiers of World War I.

Today, visitors can tour Pershing's boyhood home. Inside Prairie Mound School, a gallery leads visitors through his early childhood and his military career. A statue of "Black Jack" is surrounded by the Wall of Honor, granite tablets honoring all veterans, but especially those who served under General Pershing.

All those who recall or imagine small-town life with fondness and those who are curious about the place where a great American soldier got his start will enjoy a trip to the Pershing home in Laclede. ✳

Top: Pershing spent his youth during the 1860s and 1870s in this home. Bottom: For his service as leader of the American forces in World War I, Pershing earned the rank and title of General of the Armies, becoming the highest-ranking military officer in American history. He insisted that American troops fight under American command and later mentored many officers who became generals in World War II, including Dwight D. Eisenhower. *Both Stephanie Sidoti*

NATIONAL HISTORIC LANDMARK

Pershing's career spanned from wars with American Indians after he graduated from West Point in 1886, including leading cavalry against Apache chief Geronimo, to the dawn of the nuclear age.

**3 acres
Linn County**

Pershing State Park

29277 MO 130, Laclede

A CHILDHOOD FRIEND of Gen. John J. Pershing remembered years later that "he knew the best places to shoot squirrels or quail, knew where to find the hazel or hickory nuts. He knew where the coolest and deepest swimming pools in the Locust, Muddy, or Turkey Creeks were." Thus, when the patriotic members of the Gen. John J. Pershing State and National Park Association pondered in 1930 how to commemorate the World War I hero from Missouri, who was still living, they quickly resolved that the most suitable memorial would be a park amidst the wilds that young Jack Pershing had loved to roam.

For the young people of Laclede in the 1870s, there was no better place for outdoor adventure than the old Canfield property just west and south of town. This sprawling ranch bordered the winding Locust Creek with its mill and its swimming and fishing holes, and it included the low ridges, tall forests, and open prairies typical of north Missouri in the 1870s. In 1930 this "Jack Pershing Country" still boasted its free-flowing stream and bottomland forest. The old Canfield tract was the obvious choice for the core of the proposed memorial park.

The Civilian Conservation Corps helped Missouri develop this park, and it opened in the summer of 1940. It is difficult to imagine a more fitting memorial to the spirit of Gen. John J. Pershing than to preserve a portion of the environment that shaped him in his youth. The march of agricultural progress across northern Missouri has now rendered this remnant

of north Missouri prairie and forest a rare jewel, surrounded by miles and miles of drainage ditches, row crops, and clipped pastures.

Within the park, newly acquired farmland is being restored to mimic former oxbows, sloughs, terraces, and other wetland topography. AmeriCorps crews worked with park staff to harvest and sow seeds of prairie and marsh species and to transplant cordgrass plugs. Several sandpiper species plus yellowlegs, bitterns, golden plovers, fish crows, and thousands of ducks have returned to the newly reclaimed areas. Park naturalists have proposed expanding the Locust Creek Natural Area to include more than one thousand acres of wet prairie and bottomland forest.

Blue-winged teal and snow geese circle the prairie in spring and fall, and snow-white flocks of pelicans rest on hidden ponds. More than two hundred species of birds have been recorded here. In September, thousands of orange monarch butterflies migrate across the prairie, drifting above sawtooth and tickseed flowers. Pershing State Park is the best place to experience the long-lost world of northern Missouri wilderness.

Today, Pershing State Park offers plentiful picnic sites on the breezy uplands above the creek as well as a shady campground. The well-manicured recreation area hosts a superb display of pink redbud in the spring, and there are several small fishing ponds. From the campground, a short trail leads down to Locust Creek, where an old gristmill and dam across the creek that provided its power were once located. The pool above the dam was a favorite swimming hole for youngsters, most likely including Jack Pershing, to cool off. Pershing the general was one of a kind, and so, too, is the park that commemorates him. *

Left: Since the wetland area of Pershing State Park has been restored, water-loving birds are a common sight here. *Missouri State Parks*
Right: A boardwalk in Pershing State Park leads through the marsh and bottomland forest to the prairie beyond. *Scott Myers*

In 1940, the year this park opened, the American War Mothers of Missouri dedicated a monument in the center of the park to American mothers, who like Pershing's, gave sons to the war.

5,362 acres
Linn County

Trails
- Boardwalk Trail (1.5 mi)
- Canfield Savanna Trail (0.4 mi)
- Locust Creek Riparian Trail (6 mi)
- Oak Ridge Trail (0.4 mi)
- Scout Lake Trail (0.3 mi)

Pomme de Terre State Park

Hwy 64B, Pittsburg

Water-skiing, fishing, swimming, canoeing, and kayaking are all popular here. *George Denniston*

BEFORE THE FIRST WHITE SETTLERS came to southwest Missouri, wandering French trappers and traders had visited and explored the area's many beautiful rivers, including one they apparently named for a tuberous plant that grew in the vicinity and fed the local American Indians. The plant might have been the widespread groundnut or American potato bean (Apios americana) or the now rare prairie turnip (Pediomelum esculentum), also known as Indian breadroot or wild potato. Potato in French is pomme de terre, which means apple of the earth, and thus a fine western Ozark river was named.

For thousands of years, American Indians lived along the river. They left evidence of their passing not only in the usual middens (refuse from their campsites), but also in some intriguing burial cairns built of stone.

What we find today at Pomme de Terre is not a river but a remarkably attractive, clear lake of some 7,800 acres dating from the 1960s, compliments of the Army Corps of Engineers. The state park at "Pommey"—as the locals know it—consists of two separate parcels, one on the Hermitage side, the other on a peninsula accessible from the south, or Pittsburg, side of the lake.

The emphasis at Pomme de Terre is on water recreation, and the park offers a setting of quiet, usually uncrowded, beauty. The two park units are separated by several miles of road and function almost independently. Each has a full set of facilities for visitors. The park has more campsites than any other Missouri state park, over 240. The Pittsburg area also offers an alternate camping experience with its fabric-covered yurts. Part of the reason that camping is popular at Pomme de Terre is the shoreline location that many of the sites enjoy—bacon seems to smell better frying here in the early morning when its aroma mixes with the fog off the lake. Both campgrounds offer nearby beaches and fine swimming.

Pomme de Terre also offers a unique fishing opportunity. Some time ago, northern muskies or muskellunge, native to the Great Lakes region, were stocked in this Ozark lake; the species survived and now provides exotic sport for those who seek this large fish. A number of real lunkers have been taken. A marina consisting of a camp store and grill offers boat, equipment, and slip rentals.

Located in the western Springfield Plateau section of the Ozarks, the land around the lake is rolling rather than mountainous, and the woodlands show the influence of the prairies of the nearby Osage Plains

to the west. Today, park staff use prescribed burning to unveil a landscape once dominated by ancient 350-year-old post oaks. The trails and picnic area of the park's south side are an outstanding outdoor classroom where each spring visitors can witness a renewal of this once widespread oak parkland, now replete with wildflowers and rich prairie grasses.

There is also a trail to the ridge-top earthen burial mounds and rock cairns of the Native Americans who occupied this area. Excavations of several of the mounds have revealed materials from the Late Woodland period (AD 500 to 1000), while materials in the rock cairns are from the later Mississippian cultural tradition.

All in all, Pomme de Terre, with its evocation of French traders and Native Americans who roamed the prairies and oak woodlands, is a pleasant park that offers an idyllic setting for a family campout. *

**735 acres
Hickory County**

Trails
- Cedar Bluff Trail (1.5 mi)
- Indian Point Trail (2.75 mi)

Prairie State Park

128 NW 150th Lane, Mindenmines

FALL MUST BE THE PRETTIEST season on the prairie. Emerald-green grasses turn brilliant orange, red, bronze, and gold. During the summer, they whisper or rustle in the wind. In fall, they rattle and toss to and fro. The land seems restless and alive, its color more intense and consuming than that of forests. Standing in a swale in the midst of this rolling sea of grass, facing the wind and knee-deep in prairie asters, you are just a speck on land that must stretch to somewhere beyond forever. And all around you, engulfed by the open skies, the annual fall pageant of the prairie begins.

First, there are the northern harriers—prairie hawks that the fall prairie attracts like a magnet. Sometimes near, sometimes far, the hawks glide low, slowly skimming over the top of the grass. Or they hover, suspended, barely cresting some windy knoll—listening. Occasionally, one dives into the grass, and a noisy flock of red-winged blackbirds or a covey of quail erupts.

Beneath the prairie hawks, the bison are in a world of their own. In fall, they are in their best condition of the year. It's also breeding season, and the bulls are touchy and cantankerous. Sometimes they fight. The ground shakes and the dust flies when two one-ton animals slam full speed into one another.

Deer seem to sprout in the openness. The early morning sun highlights them and sometimes you become aware of a collection of eyes, ears, and noses—each looking your way. But since only their heads show, motionless at the surface of that tossing, grassy sea, they look strangely suspended, almost as if the heads are rooted while the land moves around.

Beside them in the distance, a short-eared owl glides home from the hunt, and two coyote heads flash up and are gone with the blink of an eye. They reappear a little farther away, bouncing high for looks above the tall fall grasses. Overhead, shimmering white dots—pelicans—wing their way south.

Even winter is special here, with deer everywhere and coyotes howling at night. The bison in their thick wooly coats have no problem with cold, sleet, or snow.

This is the essence of Prairie State Park, one of the few places left where this tallgrass drama still unfolds so completely. And it happens not just in fall, but daily, with a progression of sights and sounds that become a song of the seasons—living visions of Missouri's natural past preserved in this park. *

Top: Spring brings the booming of prairie chickens. *Jim Rathert* Middle: The highlight of Prairie State Park lies in the simple rolling beauty of its prairies. *Missouri State Parks* • Bottom: Native bison were eliminated from Missouri in the nineteenth century but were reintroduced and now number near thirty. *Scott Myers*

Missouri's sweeping prairie panoramas were all but history when this land was acquired in the late 1970s for a park. With so few fragments left—less than 1 percent of the state's original prairie—it is difficult to imagine that a third of the state's land surface once was prairie.

3,955 acres
Barton County

Trails
- Coyote Trail (3.2 mi)
- Drover's Trail (3 mi)
- Gayfeather Trail (1.50 mi)
- Path of the Earth People Trail (2 mi)
- Path of the Sky People Trail (1.75 mi)
- Sandstone Trail (4.25 mi)

Roaring River State Park

12716 Farm Rd 2239, Cassville

IT DOESN'T "ROAR"—BUT IT ONCE DID. The spring once gushed from a cleft in the dolomite bluff, twenty million gallons daily that tumbled and cascaded over, under, and around a rocky escarpment, down to the streambed below. But in the 1930s, the Civilian Conservation Corps (CCC) built a dam in front of the cleft in the bluff, and the cascade was submerged beneath the deep, blue pool we see today. A small trickling flow from the bluff high above falls into the pool, spraying and refreshing the clumps of ferns, columbines, and mosses that line the dolomite ledges that extend into the shallow, cave-like cleft in the rock. This grotto of blue and silver water, gray rock, and delicate green ferns in quiet indirect light is as lovely a scene as any in the park system.

Many of the park's facilities were built by the CCC in the 1930s, including some of those in Camp Smokey, the park's organized group camp. A modern lodge was added in the 1990s.

Today, Roaring River is stocked regularly, and the park offers premier trout fishing in a breathtaking setting: a deep, narrow valley framed by high, forested slopes—the look of mountainous terrain. About half of the park's acres are protected as the Roaring River Hills Wild Area, a designation that will preserve the wildness and rugged character of the hills. *

4,821 acres
Barry County

Trails

- Deer Leap Trail (0.2 mi)
- Devil's Kitchen Trail (1.5 mi)
- Eagle's Nest Trail (2.75 mi)
- Fire Tower Trail (3.75 mi)
- Pibern Trail (1 mi)
- River Trail (0.7 mi)
- Spring House Trail (0.4 mi)

Historic Structures

- CCC dam, lodge, group camp, and cabins

Top: For most visitors, the central attraction is fishing for rainbow trout. A lone fisherman enjoys solitude in a morning fog. *Kyle Spradley.* Bottom: The spring emerges in a peaceful grotto. *Oliver Schuchard*

Robertsville State Park

902 State Park Rd, Robertsville

Left: Aquatic activities of almost every kind are available here at Robertsville State Park. Right: The park provides more than two miles of Meramec River frontage and water fun. *Both Missouri State Parks*

SOUTH OF A GREAT BEND in the Meramec River and just a mile upstream from the Missouri Botanical Garden's Shaw Nature Reserve is a pleasant little park. The initial 1,126-acre tract of Robertsville State Park was purchased by the Missouri Department of Natural Resources in 1979.

This land was once part of a large plantation. For much of the nineteenth century, the farm was the home of Edward James Roberts, who came to Missouri from Virginia in 1830 at the age of fourteen. Seventeen years later, he married Ann M. Robertson of St. Louis County. On their sprawling farm of more than 3,000 acres on the rich bottomland along the Meramec, they raised horses, mules, cattle, swine, wheat, corn, Irish potatoes, sweet potatoes, oats, and hay. Agricultural records show that the plantation yielded 10,000 pounds of tobacco in 1850. The 1860 census indicates that Roberts held twenty-five slaves. The Roberts family cemetery remains within the park, and some descendants of the plantation workers still reside in the vicinity.

Naturally, such a substantial landowner was active in civic affairs; Roberts served as a local tax collector and as an election judge, and he was also a master Mason. When the Frisco Railroad extended west from St. Louis, it established a station on his property, giving Roberts the opportunity to develop an all-purpose business listed as "Mill-Store-Money Lending." The station survives today as Robertsville, an unincorporated town, but the trains no longer stop. Much of his land north of the railroad remained under single ownership for years. The state bought it with the help of the Land and Water Conservation Fund from a group of investors whose plans for a resort and golf courses failed to materialize.

The Meramec River borders the tract on the north and west, while Calvey Creek forms the eastern boundary. As a floodplain landscape, Robertsville does not include dramatic topography, but in the central area of the park, a small hill rises about 160 feet above the surrounding lowlands. This hill represents an erosional remnant—often called a lost hill—formed by the changing courses of the Meramec River and Calvey Creek.

One way to really experience the Robertsville landscape is to explore the Spicebush Trail that traverses some of the park's rich, lower woods. Along with the spicebush, thick, dark hanging vines of wild grapes appear almost jungle-like in places—an atmosphere that certainly goes with the heat, humidity, and insects of midsummer. Spring is beautiful, with carpets of wildflowers and a host of forest-loving birds in full song. You'll almost surely hear the high-pitched call of the red-shouldered hawk. You'll also see native woodpeckers in the tall timber. There's even a good chance to see some wild turkeys slipping through the bottoms.

With more than two miles of frontage on the Meramec River, Robertsville has great access to the river for boating and fishing. It's also the perfect spot for a waterside picnic in the shade on a summer evening. But you'll have to experience that for yourself to know what it's really like. *

Spicebush trail, less than one mile long, passes beneath a canopy of white, pin, and bur oaks, Spicebush, a native shrub, is prominent in the understory, and autumn brings its bright red berries.

1,225 acres
Franklin County

Trails
- Spice Bush Trail (0.8 mi)
- Lost Hill Trail (2.6 mi)

Historic Structures
- The Roberts family cemetery

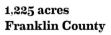

Don Robinson State Park

9275 Byrnesville Rd, Cedar Hill

Signature features at Don Robinson State Park are the many sandstone box canyons that are carved into the landscape. Over many years, water has sliced through the grainy sandstone beds to form steep canyons with some walls exceeding eighty feet in height.

818 acres
Jefferson County

Trails
• Sandstone Canyon Trail (4 mi)
• Labarque Hills Trail (2.4 mi)

Historic Structure
• Don Robinson's home

IN THE RUGGED LABARQUE CREEK HILLS is one of the newest jewels in the state park system. Don Robinson assembled a personal retreat over the years since his initial purchase in 1964, and then he willed them to the people of Missouri as a park upon his passing in March 2012. With an estimated value of more than $5 million, the land is among the largest gifts in the century-long history of our state parks.

Robinson was struck by the ruggedness of the surrounding landscape when he bought his first 320-acre parcel in 1964. Fondly recalling his first visit, he explained, "It was so cold out the beer was freezing on top of the cans. I thought, well, this is really pre-historic—I just gotta get it." As he continued to add adjacent parcels, he realized he was getting close to a tract the size of New York City's famed Central Park, which has 843 acres, and at that he stopped.

Robinson's home, where he lived alone for nearly half a century, sits on one of the most striking vistas of the park. He described it as "just a cut above camping—but I like it that way." The lower stone portion of the house had been built in 1928, but he added a second floor and, later, a clerestory of his own design. One change he never made to the house was adding a finished ground floor—the floor was literally the bedrock knoll on which the house sat. In 1997 an elaborate treehouse in his woods graced the cover of *Smithsonian* magazine. The treehouse no longer survives.

Several tributaries of LaBarque Creek—French for "the boat"—originate in the park. With forty-four species of fish, it is considered one of the highest quality streams in the St. Louis area. Less than forty miles from downtown St. Louis, Robinson's land includes outcroppings of limestone, dolomite, and sandstone that give rise to a rich mosaic of ecosystems. The St. Peter sandstone has been sculpted into dry open glades, moist box canyons, cliffs, waterfalls, chutes, pools, and overhangs. The park has impressive botanical diversity and outstanding bird and wildlife resources, too.

Don Robinson decided that Missouri State Parks would fulfill his vision of preserving this beautiful landscape for future generations to enjoy. On a peaceful knoll just a short walk from his former home, he rests for eternity, having become a part of the wild acres he so loved. *

Top: Don Robinson's home showcases his architectural interests. *Susan Flader* • Middle: Several overhangs sculpted in St. Peter sandstone harbor mosses, lichens, liverworts, and in winter, icicles, and so are beautiful in every season. *Ron Colatskie* • Bottom: This waterfall spills down into a sandstone box canyon. *Allison Vaughn*

Rock Bridge Memorial State Park

5901 S Hwy 163, Columbia

BECAUSE OF ITS ODDITY, this area south of Columbia was probably destined to become a state park, if not preserved in some other way, although this is hindsight, of course. There are so many natural phenomena here to excite human curiosity. Flowing creeks disappear underground. Natural shallow ponds called sinkholes act like funnels, holding water for only a short time after heavy rains. Deep holes in the earth open into extensive caverns. Bats boil out of these caves at dusk. There's a spectacular chasm where a stream emerges from the foot of one cliff only to flow toward another one and beneath a massive arch of limestone topped by trees. This is the centerpiece, the rock bridge that gave the park its name. All are characteristics of a karst landscape underlain by porous and water-soluble limestone.

Despite the challenges of accommodating a growing regional population, Rock Bridge is a delightful destination. Countless fond memories of this park derive from springtime visits by students from the nearby universities; something draws young people when the air softens, wildflowers blossom, and birds call from greening woodlands. Try a picnic near the natural bridge followed by exploration of the trails. Listen for spring peepers, watch for Virginia bluebells, and catch the fragrance of wild plum. ✳

Top: Devil's Ice Box Spring Branch trickles under the natural bridge that gives this park its name, and exploring its underside is one of the many joys that await visitors. *Katelyn Johnson* • Bottom: Special guided tours of the cave and park teach children about nature. These Boy Scouts explore nooks and crannies. *Missouri State Parks*

**2,273 acres
Boone County**

Trails
- Deer Run Trail (3.8 mi)
- Devil's Icebox Trail (0.5 mi)
- Gans Creek Wild Area Trail System (6.6 mi)
- Grassland Trail (1.9 mi)
- High Ridge Trail (1.75)
- Karst Trail (1.9 mi)
- Sinkhole Trail (1.4 mi)
- Spring Brook Trail (3.1 mi)

Rock Island Spur of Katy Trail State Park

Various trailheads

Chicago, Rock Island and Pacific Railroad

THE CHICAGO, ROCK ISLAND, and Pacific Railroad, commonly called the Rock Island Line, provided the trail that stretches 47.5 miles through the heart of west-central Missouri and adventure for bicyclists, hikers, and horseback riders. The trail takes users between Windsor and Pleasant Hill, with additional trailheads at Leeton, Chilhowee, and Medford along the way.

The Rock Island Line was sometimes described as "one railroad too many" in the late nineteenth and early twentieth centuries. It began operations in 1852 as the Chicago and Rock Island Railroad, operating trains between those two Illinois cities. With transcontinental aspirations, the company later stretched across Missouri as far west as Kansas, Nebraska, Colorado, New Mexico, Oklahoma, and Texas, but it never made it to the Pacific. The Rock Island seemed to have left early but arrived late, as its expansions tended to bring it into head-to-head competition with well-established rail lines that had more direct routes, leaving the Rock Island to build over less favorable terrain and more circuitous routes.

Left: When the Rock Island reached Windsor in 1904, it passed beneath the already existing Katy Railroad. This bridge and underpass is now the junction of the Katy Trail with the Rock Island Trail, as the Katy heads southwest to Clinton and the Rock Island heads west to Kansas City. *Ben Nickelson* • Right: The trail passes along a lake where steam locomotives once refilled their boilers. *Tom Uhlenbrock*

The route of Rock Island's original tracks from St. Louis to Kansas City was constructed through some of the state's most rugged topography, including several river crossings, which required multiple feats of engineering prowess to complete.

47 miles, with more to come

Cass, Henry, and Johnson Counties

But what was challenging for the builders delivers beauty to trail users today, as the trail passes through prairie-like landscapes, picturesque farm fields, and dense woodlands while crossing numerous streams. The trail is a designated section of the nationwide American Discovery Trail, a coast-to-coast nonmotorized recreational trail.

This section of the railroad traveled through farm fields and grazing land punctuated with coal-mining operations, and the railroad carried shipments of grain, vegetables, other agricultural products, and coal. Travelers on the old line might have recognized Windsor was named for Windsor Castle and looked out the window on small communities they passed through, such as Bowen, New Castle, Leeton, Post Oak, Chilhowee (a Cherokee name), Denton, Medford, Hadsell, and Wingate before arriving at Pleasant Hill, named for its "pleasant situation on an elevated prairie."

Rock Island Trail State Park can be enjoyed on its own or as part of a much longer trail ride. At Windsor, the trail connects to Katy Trail State Park. Combining the trails gives riders or hikers the chance to go from Pleasant Hill, part of the greater Kansas City area, to Machens, part of the greater St. Louis area.

The time has come again when, as the old American folk song says: "The Rock Island Line is a mighty good road; The Rock Island Line is the road to ride." ✳

Route 66 State Park

97 N Outer Rd, Eureka

NO OTHER UNIT of the Missouri state park system has had so strange a genesis as Route 66 State Park. A newspaper publicity stunt gave birth to a town that eventually was crossed by America's famous "Mother Road," and then a flood and an environmental disaster wiped out the town.

The town of Times Beach blossomed out of the "Greatest Subscription Offer Ever Made." That was the front-page headline in *The St. Louis Times* on July 25, 1925. With the purchase of a six-month subscription to the paper, the buyer could also purchase a 20-by-100-foot building lot for only $67.50 ($10 down, $2.50 monthly) in the "new summer resort developed by the newspaper for its readers." All lots would have equal rights to the beach on a beautiful stretch of the Meramec River, a riverfront park, and membership in a community lodge. At first, the owners of the new lots built mainly fishing shacks and small cabins, often on stilts in case of floods.

Then in 1933 one of the principal radial streets became the corridor through town for the newly designated Highway 66, headed for Los Angeles. The town continued to grow, and by the 1970 census, there were several hundred houses, two trailer courts, and over two thousand residents—although no paved streets. In 1972 and 1973, the city arranged to have the streets sprayed with waste oil, to suppress dust from the gravel streets and dirt lanes.

Then calamity struck. Ten inches of rain in four days created a massive flood in 1982, huge beyond any previous expectation. The December crest of twenty-four feet above flood stage on the Meramec inundated the entire town from one end to the other. At nearly the same time, the Environmental Protection Agency (EPA) confirmed that the waste oil sprayed on the streets ten years earlier had been contaminated with potentially deadly amounts of dioxin.

Officials determined that the best method for disposal of dioxin and the contaminated soil and other material was high temperature incineration. At extreme temperatures, dioxin, an organic compound, decomposes into a harmless residue of ash. Today, these ash mounds that resulted have settled and compacted so much that they barely register as mounds. Alongside one straight run of park road is a peculiar earthen structure, twelve or fifteen feet high and thirty feet wide, grass covered, and stretching a quarter-mile along the road. It is an interesting landscape feature, mimicking an Etruscan tumulus or a Native American burial mound, and containing all that remains of the city of Times Beach, mashed, compacted, and safely interred. It is ironically known as the town mound. The land has reverted to nature once again and is one

Find a Route 66 special edition motorcycle and a Phillips 66 sign in the 1935 roadhouse that is now the park's visitor center and Route 66 Museum. The visitor center explains the story of Times Beach. *Don Fink*

of the most popular parks in the St. Louis area. The park abounds with opportunities to bike, walk, and bird-watch.

A roadhouse along Route 66, built in 1935, serves as the park's visitor center. This roadhouse comes alive with the memories of many travelers who visited it during the Route 66 era and ate at the restaurant, which was known for its marvelous food. Depending on the year of visit, the roadhouse had four different owners. It opened as the Bridgehead Inn in 1935; Steiny's Inn in 1946; Bridgehead Inn in 1972; and the Galley West in 1980.

The visitor center has displays of Route 66 memorabilia and souvenirs. A gift shop in the center has hundreds of Route 66 items and is open seven days a week from March through November.

An area once considered a disaster now lures Route 66 fans and has turned into an inviting park enjoyed by hundreds of thousands of visitors annually. ✳

424 acres
St. Louis County

Trails
- Inner Loop Trail (2 mi)
- Outer Loop Trail (3.25 mi)
- South Loop Trail (1.5 mi)
- W Trail (0.5 mi)

Historic Structures
- Route 66 bridge and roadhouse
- The Town Mound

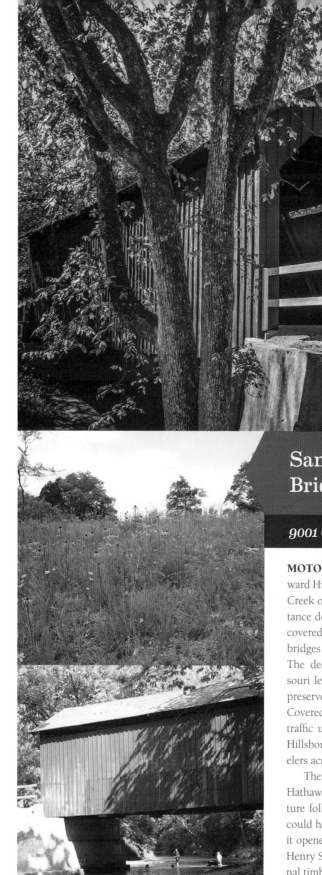

Sandy Creek Covered Bridge State Historic Site

9001 Old Lemay Ferry Rd, Hillsboro

MOTORISTS HEADING SOUTH from St. Louis toward Hillsboro may not realize when they cross Sandy Creek on State Route 21 that located just a short distance downstream is one of Missouri's last remaining covered bridges. Once fairly numerous, the covered bridges still standing numbered only eleven by 1942. The decline continued until 1967, when the Missouri legislature authorized the state park system to preserve the four remaining structures. Sandy Creek Covered Bridge, originally built in 1872, still carried traffic until 1984. The bridge is located on the old Hillsboro-Lemay Ferry Road, where a ferry took travelers across the creek before the bridge was built.

The bridge was constructed of white pine by John Hathaway Morse for $2,000. The 76-foot-long structure followed the Howe truss design and reportedly could handle up to seventy tons. Fourteen years after it opened, it was destroyed during spring floods. But Henry Steffin was able to salvage about half the original timbers and rebuild the bridge for only $889.

No formal trail system leads into the Fort Hill area of the site, but visitors can explore it on short hikes of their own. With a lunch in the creek-side picnic area, a stroll through the old bridge, and a hike into the woods, this small historic site can provide all the requirements for whiling away a lazy afternoon. *

Sandy Creek took its name from the St. Peter sandstone exposed along the the south-facing slope of a long ridge south of the creek, known locally as both Sandy Ridge or Sand Ridge.

**212 acres
Jefferson County**

Top: The covered bridge provides a bright focal point during any season. *Jim Diaz* • Middle: Glade coneflowers and coreopsis adorn nearby Fort Hill, a short hike from the bridge. *Missouri State Parks* Bottom: Wading in the creek below the bridge and a deeply shaded picnic area are popular on hot summer days. *George Denniston*

Sappington Cemetery State Historic Site

Co Rd AA, Nelson

THE HUGE RED CEDARS ARE VISIBLE for a quarter-mile before you arrive at Sappington Cemetery, five miles west of Arrow Rock in Saline County. These magnificent trees were greatly beloved by the pioneers, not only for their associations with scriptural passages, but also as an evergreen reminder of the promise of everlasting life in an otherwise deciduous world. Nearly every pioneer home had one or more in the yard, and every old cemetery in Missouri featured them. They are frequently older than the houses they are standing by, and these at Sappington Cemetery are perhaps older than the first burial. The largest is over two and a half feet in diameter.

Thomas Gray, in his famous "Elegy Written in a Country Churchyard" of 1750, fixed forever in our consciousness the sense of romance and history embodied, literally, in a country burying ground:

> The lowing herd wind slowly o'er the lea,
> The plowman homeward plods his weary way,
> And leaves the world to darkness and to me.

Gray's words perfectly describe a visit to Sappington Cemetery. Even today, when your eye strays away from the limestone-walled enclosure, through the small grove surrounding it, and onto the high rolling prairie beyond, you see a scene of bucolic peace, the grassland studded with grazing cattle.

Dr. John Sappington (1776-1856), after whom the cemetery is named, was a celebrity of his day, not only as Southern gentry but for developing quinine pills to treat malaria. For several decades, he was a power broker of the Central Clique, the so-called "Boone's Lick Democracy," that controlled Missouri politics for most of the first half of the nineteenth century. Two of his sons-in-law, who lie nearby, and one grandson became governors of the state.

Visit the cemetery and the nearby Sappington African American (formerly known as Negro) Cemetery on a Sunday afternoon in mid-November. You will likely have them entirely to yourself and not hear a sound other than the rustling of the dry but not yet fallen oak leaves and the swooshing of the breeze passing through the red cedars. The low angle of the autumnal sun will heighten the melancholy air of the cemeteries. Here, in these special places, a sense of life in the old Missouri Boone's Lick country is palpable. ✳

Top: Gov. Claiborne Fox Jackson was reinterred here after the Civil War. *Oliver Schuchard* • Bottom: Near the main cemetery lies Sappington Negro Cemetery, a vital part of the record and interpretation of black heritage in Arrow Rock. *Michael Dickey*

Claiborne Fox Jackson (1806-1862), Missouri's fifteenth governor and the leader of Missouri's pro-Confederate government, died in exile in Arkansas. He had married three daughters of John Sappington, the first two having died young. His remains were reinterred here after the war ended.

4 acres
Saline County

St. Francois State Park

8920 US 67, Bonne Terre

Hikers explore the Pike Run Trail, which crosses much of the Coonville Creek Wild Area and showcases the type of undeveloped, landscapes characteristic of state park wild areas. *Scott Myers*

DESCRIBING HIS HIDE-OUT during the Civil War, in the Pike Run Hills of St. Francois County, Sam Hildebrand in 1870 is reported to have said, "They look like the fragments of a broken up world piled together in dread confusion, and terminating finally in an abrupt bluff on the margin of Big River."

St. Francois State Park is named for the county in which it is located, not for the ancient mountains just to the south. The park is a superlative example of the intricately dissected topography so characteristic of this part of Missouri, especially along the larger streams. The underlying bedrock has been carved over millennia by water draining to the Big River. The resulting hills and hollows are cloaked in forests and woodlands of oak, hickory, and red cedar, with several glade openings on south-facing slopes.

The soul of this landscape and the setting for its most exciting natural features is the valley of Coonville Creek; an inviting trail leads up the valley. One of the first things that will strike you about this small stream is the clarity of its waters. Another will be the beauty of its musical flow over bedrock ledges, not rushing and turbulent in normal seasons, but gentle and refreshing. Pausing at one of the many pools, you can lose yourself in the aquarium-like world of graceful native fish, aquatic insects, and delicately floating leaves. Over eighteen kinds of fish live here, including the colorful southern redbelly dace, the orangethroat darter, and the nocturnal slender madtom.

Along the valley, the trail passes a number of small springs and seeps. These cool, dependable waters help account for the steady clear flow of the stream. Around some of the seeps, boggy soils support plant communities called fens. Growing in these fens are botanical rarities such as the grass pink orchid, swamp wood betony, and swamp thistle. The rarest jewel in this valley is the queen of the prairie, with its luxuriant deep green foliage and tall summer-flowering spikes bearing dense clusters of pink blossoms. All of these features render Coonville Creek one of the premier small streams in the Ozarks. It has been designated an Outstanding State Resource Water for its aesthetic and scientific value, and its valley is the Coonville Creek Natural Area. But Coonville wears its titles lightly. It is a friendly stream that will call you again and again to wander in its valley and along its banks.

In the early twentieth century, the narrow hollows and coves of these hills proved ideal for the time-honored Ozark custom of making moonshine whiskey. The remoteness today offers other values. Up one of the side hollows off Coonville Creek, a lovely spring emerges from a shaded, mossy grotto. Moist ledges glisten with ferns and liverworts. Dogwood branches and wild hydrangeas nod overhead, and the gurgle of spring water over shiny pebbles soothes the ear.

St. Francois State Park provides an immaculately kept campground and lovely picnic sites, and the Big River provides wading and swimming holes as well as easy canoeing. More than 80 percent of the park has been designated the Coonville Creek Wild Area, accessible via the ten-mile Pike Run Trail. Park visitors can enjoy an outstanding interpretive program and many activities.

Whether your interest is natural history and you enjoy the unusual local plants, animals, and geology, or your imagination is fired by the lonely vigils of Sam Hildebrand and others hiding in these ancient hills, St. Francois State Park is waiting to welcome you and your family to your own refuge, a place of exploration and refreshment. ✳

2,735 acres
St. Francois County

Trails

- Mooner's Hollow Trail (2.75 mi)
- Pike Run Trail (south loop, 6.25 mi and north loop, 4 mi)
- Swimming Deer Trail (3.15 mi)

St. Joe State Park

2800 Pimville Rd, Park Hills

WHEN ST. JOE MINERALS corporation shut down its great lead-processing mill at Flat River in 1972, having largely exhausted nearby ore deposits, the future of the mined-out area had been forecast by popular usage. Enthusiasts of the new and versatile off-road vehicles (ORVs)—dune buggies, all-terrain vehicles (ATVs), and motorcycles—found a challenging playground in the hundreds of acres of tailings, crushed limestone from which lead was extracted, that formed a desert-like surface. Company officials donated this area along with more land for a park.

Thus, Missouri acquired a highly diverse recreational area accommodating many different uses. The The ORV riding area at St. Joe is made up of about 800 acres of tailings and 1,200 acres of wooded slopes. Riders even have a designated campground with direct access to the trails. Eleven miles of paved bicycle and hiking trails offer access to the park's diverse landscapes. Several other hiking, biking, and horse trails traverse more than seventeen miles of rugged oak and hickory woods. Mountain biking is growing, too. Four small clear-water lakes invite anglers, and two of the lakes have excellent swimming beaches.

From its not-so-propitious beginnings as a lead mining area, the park has developed into a beautiful, safe, enjoyable haven for family recreation. *

St. Joe is one of the best off-road vehicle areas in the Midwest and Missouri's fourth-largest state park. You can also hike, bike, and ride horses here.

8,243 acres
St. Francois County

Trails
- Hickory Ridge Trail (4 mi)
- Lakeview Trail (1.25 mi)
- ORV Trail System (30 mi)
- Paved Bicycle Trail (11 mi)
- Pine Ridge Trail (12.6 mi)

Top: ORV enthusiasts, well over half of them in family groups, make up most of the park's 600,000 plus annual visitors and probably always will. *Missouri State Parks* • Bottom: Naturalists have learned that significant stands of native shortleaf pine and oak woodlands in the eastern and southern parts of the park are the most botanically diverse of any native woodlands in Missouri parks. *Ron Colatskie*

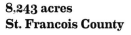

Stockton State Park

19100 Hwy 215, Dadeville

Many claim that Stockton Lake offers the best sailing in the lower Midwest. The key is the steady southwest breeze off the Springfield Plateau that sweeps over 25,000 acres of clear, open water.

**2,176 acres
Cedar County**

Trails
- Nyblad Trail (0.5 mi)
- Lake View Trail (8 mi)
- Umber Ridge Trail (1.65 mi)
- Water Trail (6.7 mi)

FRESHWATER SAILORS pursue the sport here in southwest Missouri at Stockton Lake, an Army Corps of Engineers reservoir. Sailing may not be the most common water recreation in Missouri, but the lake's ultra-clear waters and wooded shorelines lure sailors from Missouri and neighboring states.

Headquarters for most Stockton sailors is Stockton State Park, leased from the corps and developed for recreation by the state of Missouri. The full-service marina welcomes visitors. In addition to the traditional campgrounds and picnic areas, the park also offers a camp store, a restaurant on the dock, and several lodging options ranging from duplexes with kitchens to rustic camper cabins.

Beyond sailing, the park is popular with recreational boaters and lake fishermen, who enjoy the unspoiled shoreline and elbow-room on the uncrowded lake. Canoeists and kayakers can spend their time paddling the park's seven-mile water trail along the shore of a cliff-lined peninsula, with launch points on either side only a mile apart. The park also offers hiking and biking trails that wind through oak and hickory woodlands, with spectacular views of the lake.

The park is located on a long north-south peninsula once known as Umber Point, a prominent ridge dividing the valleys of the Sac and Little Sac Rivers. This western Springfield plateau region of the Ozarks is not as shady as some other places, being a transition zone for prairie, savanna, and open woodland.

Extensive archaeology performed in conjunction with the reservoir construction project in the 1960s revealed this area to have a complex prehistory, but one typical of the rest of the Osage River basin. There is evidence of human occupation for at least ten thousand years, with changing ways of life as climate and vegetation changed over time. This was Osage country when French explorers first learned of it in the seventeenth century, but the Cherokee, Chickasaw, and Choctaw from the Southeast moved into the region late in the next century.

Since the Civil War, the biggest event in this county by far has been the construction of Stockton Lake. Authorized by the Flood Control Act of 1954 for that purpose and to provide power, water supply, and recreation, the dam across Sac River was completed in 1972. Since then, the Sac and Little Sac Rivers have formed one of the clearest lakes in the state. *

Top: Sailboats brighten the breezy waters at Stockton Lake. Middle: Kayakers enjoy the water trail around Umber Point, with many quiet covers and places for swimming and fishing. *Both Missouri State Parks* • Bottom: Three hiking trails offer almost ten miles of hiking for off-the-water fun and exercise. *Scott Myers*

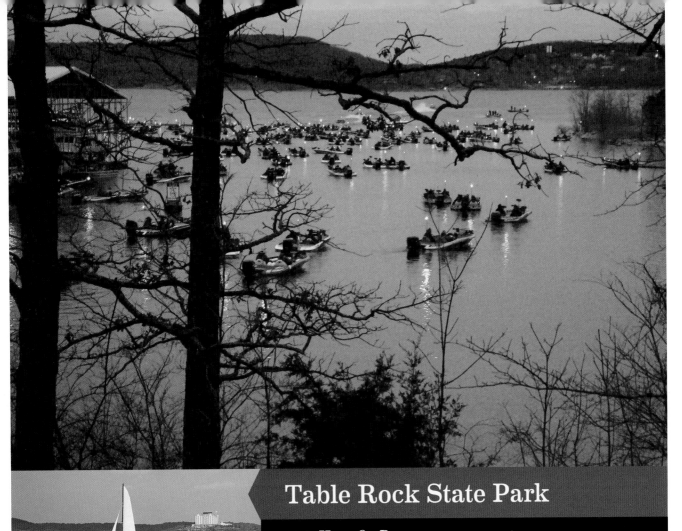

Table Rock State Park

5272 Hwy 165, Branson

VOTED THE BEST PARK in the Midwest by a near-ly two-to-one margin by readers of the *AAA Midwest Traveler* magazine in 2010, Table Rock State Park provides a nature break from all the bustle of Branson. Many visitors to the park are attracted by abundant entertainment in the vicinity, but they clearly appreciate what the park itself has to offer.

The lake is also a perennial favorite among boat enthusiasts and anglers, who revere it for the crystal clarity of its waters, and it has the largest full-service marina at any state park. You can rent a boat, grab a bite to eat, take a tour of the lake, or even rent a bike at the marina, awarded Missouri's first "Clean Marina" designation. While you're visiting the park, take a naturalist-led walk or attend an evening program.

The lake was created when the Army Corps of Engineers built Table Rock Dam, by far the highest in the state at 252 feet, on the White River, in the storied *Shepherd of the Hills* region. Harold Bell Wright's best-selling book can be credited with the first wave of tourism to the area.

You'll find a refreshing and scenic experience awaiting you here. Try your luck at fishing in the clear waters, go for a swim in the summer months, or find along some backwoods trail much that is still unspoiled and inviting in the White River Hills. ✳

356 acres
Stone and Taney
Counties

Trails
- Chinquapin Trail (1.2 mi)
- Table Rock Lakeshore Trail (2.45 mi)
- White River Valley Trail System (11.3 mi)

Top: The park annually attracts one million visitors from across Missouri and the country. *Carl Bonnell* • Middle: You can rent a boat to enjoy the crystal waters, rocky shores, and surrounding hills of the lake. *Missouri State Parks* Bottom: Mountain bikers navigate the White River Trail. *Carl Bonnell*

Taum Sauk Mountain State Park

148 Taum Sauk Trail, Middle Brook

A lichen-covered igneous glade on the west flank of Taum Sauk Mountain overlooks Taum Sauk valley. This park is important for songbirds that depend on large undisturbed forest areas. *Ron Colatskie*

THE GEOLOGIC PHOENIX of the Ozarks, Taum Sauk Mountain was born of volcanic fire 1.5 billion years ago, then rose eons later at the very center of the Ozark dome. If Elephant Rocks is where one goes into the core of the Ozarks amid the pink granite boulders, Taum Sauk is where one ascends to the apex of the Ozark dome and surveys the world around. Located at the center of the 5,000-square-mile St. Francois Mountains with thirty nearby summits, Taum Sauk—likely a reference to the Sauk tribe, possibly meaning Big Sauk—is the state's highest point at 1,772 feet above sea level. Nowhere else in Missouri does such a panorama of nature's wild treasures and earthly forces combine.

A short spur off the popular Mina Sauk Falls Trail takes you up to Missouri's highest point. At the summit, the mountain is flat. While its height is not sufficient to demonstrate life zones at different elevations, its height above the surrounding Ozark plateau teases the atmosphere enough to show subtle climatic differences. While the summer temperature on top of the mountain often reaches ninety degrees Fahrenheit, winter's weather is like that of Kirksville in northeastern Missouri, and local residents may witness the mountaintops capped in snow. All around, tree limbs lie scattered about the mountain crest, having shattered under the weight of frequent ice storms. Nearly every tree shows the influence of wind and ice breakage and the scars of lightning strikes.

Then take the three-mile-loop trail to the Mina Sauk Falls, which gradually descends the mountain's west flank onto successive glades of exposed igneous rock, here and there dotted by dwarfed trees and grasses resulting from the shallow, droughty soils. Smoke and Church mountains loom through the veil of a low cloud cap south of the Taum Sauk Creek valley. To the north are Wildcat Mountain and Weimer Hill, and in the distance, the northeast-trending arc of Proffit Mountain; their summits fall just short of the highest point on Taum Sauk. This is one of few vantage points from which one can see a portion of the high white wall of Ameren's Taum Sauk hydroelectric storage reservoir—located at the southern end of Proffit Mountain. Your attention may be pleasantly diverted by a pair of turkey vultures riding fixed on an invisible wave of mountain air.

After about four hundred feet of progressively steeper descent from the top of Taum Sauk, a timeless roar signals that Mina Sauk Falls is near. At the crest of the falls, rainwater collects in a small stream before plunging down a series of volcanic rock ledges positioned at right angles across ancient faults and rock fractures. The total drop of the falls is 132 feet, making this Missouri's tallest wet weather waterfall. Here, you can gaze with wonder at the massive knobs on each side of the deep valley below. The pink-layered rock underlying the falls is ash that spewed forth from some ancient volcano more than a billion years ago.

Taum Sauk Mountain State Park offers unsurpassed scenery, genuine backcountry, delicate igneous barrens, an unspoiled headwaters creek, and diverse woodlands. Well-known to Boy Scouts for more than half a century, as they traversed the former 28-mile Taum Sauk Boy Scout Trail from Elephant Rocks to Taum Sauk Mountain, this extraordinary mountain landscape lies at the geologic heart of the Ozarks. That trail no longer officially exisits as parts have been removed to follow the direct route of the Ozark Trail. Hike along trails deep into the wilds, or admire and enjoy the views from roadside overlooks. *

9,628 acres
Iron and Reynolds Counties

Trails
- Mina Sauk Falls Trail (3 mi)
- Taum Sauk Section of the Ozark Trail (14.5 mi)

Thousand Hills State Park

20431 Rt 157, Kirksville

KIRKSVILLE FACED CHALLENGES in the years following World War II. The northeast Missouri community needed fresh clean water for a population that had more than doubled since 1900, and they needed to provide outdoor recreation opportunities for that same population. The two problems seem related, and the town leaders knew they had some advantages. There was Big Creek, a large stream west of town that flowed through wooded, hilly land. There was lively interest in bringing some of the benefits of public recreation land to this portion of the state. And there was the legacy of Dr. George Mark Laughlin.

George Laughlin moved to Kirksville to study osteopathic medicine with Dr. A. T. Still. Laughlin flourished in his endeavors and married Still's daughter. In addition to medicine, Laughlin had an interest in land, and he eventually developed a large farm west of town that he called Thousand Hills Farm.

Laughlin died in 1948, and the following year Kirksville leaders conceived a solution to both of their problems—a large freshwater lake on Big Creek in the rugged Thousand Hills country. The Laughlin heirs concurred with the plan and donated 1,000 acres of the old farm. The city raised funds to buy another 1,500 acres. By 1952, the 600-acre Forest Lake reservoir was completed. Then the whole tract was turned over to the state for a park. The city retained ownership of the lake to ensure their water supply. Most

of the original facilities at Thousand Hills State Park were built between 1955 and 1964.

The park is centered around Forest Lake with its seventeen miles of shoreline, and many of the activities here are on or in the water. A marina provides boat rentals and supplies. Fishing and swimming are good, and so is bird-watching along the shore. Fully furnished cabins are available, if you are not in the mood to camp.

You will also want to visit the petroglyphs and walk the trails. The petroglyphs are enclosed in a shelter for protection against vandalism and the elements, but windows along an outside ramp allow you to view them even when the building is not open. If you are adventurous, take the rugged, ten-mile Thousand Hills Trail, which nearly encircles the lake and wanders through hundreds of acres of oak woodland and savanna. Northern Missouri was once more than half savanna and prairie. Few remnants remain, so park naturalists have been restoring and managing these at Thousand Hills with prescribed fire. The trail also takes you into an isolated little valley where a rare tree grows. The large-toothed aspen is a northern species, and most of its range is far to the north. But a small colony of this beautiful and delicate visitor grows in protected seclusion here at Thousand Hills.

Wildlife abounds in the park. Deer, turkey, red fox, coyotes, barred and great-horned owls, and various ducks are fairly easy to see if you know when to expect them, and other rarer species like bald eagles and ospreys occasionally appear. Speak to the park naturalist to help make your visit really special.

Thousand Hills is a unique state park with its mission shared between Kirksville and the state. It benefits both the city and the people of Missouri. *

Left: The shelter protects highly realistic rock carvings of deer, opossums, snakes, lizards, and at least four different birds, likely by people of the Late Woodland period, around AD 400 to 900. *George Denniston* • Right: Forest Lake has a marina where you can rent boats and buy supplies and enjoy fishing, swimming, hiking, and bird-watching along the seventeen miles of shoreline. *Oliver Schuchard*

A dining lodge was built on a lovely spot overlooking Forest Lake. This lodge has developed into one of the finest restaurants in northeast Missouri, with a reputation for excellent food and a beautiful setting.

3,079 acres
Adair County

Trails
- Forest Lake (0.6 mi)
- Oak Trail (0.2 mi)
- Red Bud Trail (1.25 mi)
- Thousand Hills Trail (10.5 mi)

Towosahgy State Historic Site

County Rd 502, East Prairie

THE MOUND BUILDERS INSPIRED a life-long curiosity in Thomas Beckwith, born in 1840 on a farm in the Missouri Bootheel. The prehistoric people were called Mound Builders because their villages featured large earthen mounds. The site of one of the largest of these villages was situated on one of Thomas Beckwith's farms. Located on a ridge of sand known as Pinhook Ridge, the ancient village was bordered on one side by an extinct channel of the Mississippi River. The site was known as Beckwith's Fort, and Beckwith himself had dug extensively.

Today, these Native Americans builders are known as part of the Mississippian cultural tradition that spread up and down the river from its center at Cahokia, Illinois. Their villages were found throughout the southeastern United States, and especially in the Mississippi River valley.

At the urging of Dr. Carl Chapman of the University of Missouri, the State Park Board purchased the site in 1967, with grant assistance from the Land and Water Conservation Fund. At Chapman's suggestion, the park was named Towosahgy, a word borrowed from the Osage language meaning "old town."

Given his passion for Missouri's mound builders, Beckwith would likely be pleased to know that his mounds are now permanently preserved. *

The large ceremonial mound on the north end of the plaza in this village was over 250 feet long, and still stands to this day a full 16 feet high—built of many tons of soil moved by hand labor from a nearby borrow pit.

**64 acres
Mississippi County**

Top: This humble hill is the largest of Towosahgy's mounds. The Mound Builders were urban dwellers and conducted various ceremonies upon it until about AD 1420. *Oliver Schuchard* • Bottom: Visitors climb the temple mound at Towosahgy. *Missouri State Parks*

Trail of Tears State Park

429 Moccasin Springs Rd, Jackson

THE VIEW FROM THE OVERLOOK is grand and serene. The Mississippi River stretches lazily north and south. Limestone bluffs two hundred feet high stand guard on the west, and bottomland farms line the eastern side of the valley. You may spot an eagle soaring over the forest that cloaks the rugged hollows that extend through the bluffs to the river.

Regardless of the peaceful vision this sublime view may evoke, it once overlooked one of the saddest episodes in American history. That infamy gives Trail of Tears State Park its name. Here at Moccasin Springs in the fall and winter of 1838 and 1839, nine contingents of Cherokee were ferried across the icy Mississippi River, a formidable obstacle on the forced march from their Appalachian homeland to a new home in Indian Territory in what know today as Oklahoma.

The park's extensive forests, despite some early logging, resemble the great woods of the Cherokee homeland. Trail of Tears State Park preserves Missouri's best sizable example of what botanists call "western mesophytic" forest. Mesophytic refers to the relative moisture in the soil. Here on the deeper, richer soils protected in the cove ravines along the river, growing conditions mirror those of the Appalachian Mountains to the east.

Perhaps the Cherokee viewed this rugged terrain and dense forest with longing, as it resembled the homeland they were forced to leave. From the Mississippi, the Cherokee took three routes across Missouri; portions have been marked as part of the Trail of Tears National Historic Trail, established in 1987. Roughly one of every four Cherokee died in holding stockades or during the forced migration. The remainder arrived a broken and politically divided people. In spite of everything, the Cherokee built a remarkable society in their new homeland and continue to thrive as a nation within a nation.

Trail of Tears State Park was a gift to the state by the people of Cape Girardeau County, who authorized a $150,000 bond to purchase more than 3,000 acres in 1956. A handsome visitor center provides exhibits on the natural history of the park and on the Cherokee tragedy. The park is a superb preserve of an original Mississippi River landscape. It is also a sober reminder of the intolerance of a young country and a memorial to a resilient people who persevered. ∗

Top: Thousands of Cherokee were ferried across this section of the Mississippi River and camped near here during the harsh winter of 1838 to 1839 on the infamous Trail of Tears. *Denise Dowling* • Middle: Vistas stop hikers in their tracks. *George Denniston* • Bottom: A steamboat reminds us of other histories from this region. *Missouri State Parks*

The park features trees of greater size and variety. Oaks abound, but they join many typically Eastern species such as tulip poplar, cucumber magnolia, and American beech. A small parasitic plant called "beech drops" can be found around some beech tree roots. You may also see the rare pennywort, a delicate plant that flowers early in the spring.

**3,415 acres
Cape Girardeau
County**

Trails
- Lake Trail (2.25 mi)
- Nature Trail (0.6 mi)
- Peewah Trail (9 mi)
- Sheppard Point Trail (3 mi)

Trails of the Roger Pryor Pioneer Backcountry

County Rd 19-250, Salem

DEEP IN THE OZARKS, the region surrounding the Current River includes the most extensive forests and some of the most rugged topography in the state. At more than 140,000 acres, Pioneer Forest is the largest holding of private land in Missouri, and it is owned by the L-A-D Foundation. Of that forest, the most expansive and primitive block of 62,000 acres is designated as the Roger Pryor Pioneer Backcountry, comprised of miles of wooded, hilly country, all draining to the Current River by way of three unspoiled streams.

In the early 1950s, Leo A. Drey began to acquire the Ozark lands that became Pioneer Forest. These lands, like much of the Ozarks, had been logged heavily and were in poor condition. Drey's resolve was to restore them to health and productivity, and he sought advice from various professionals, especially foresters and conservationists. One of Leo Drey's advisors regarding environmental issues was another St. Louisan named R. Roger Pryor. Shortly after his untimely death in 1999 at age fifty-four, Drey selected the largest contiguous block of Pioneer Forest and designated it as the Roger Pryor Pioneer Backcountry.

Part of Drey's vision included a trail system that provides access to a remote setting as far removed from modern surroundings as one can get in Missouri. The Backcountry remains a working forest, but it is primitive and even isolated, a place where one must be observant and careful to avoid getting lost. Here is a landscape that is undeveloped, unconfined,

Left: The remoteness here is unsurpassed in Missouri's park system. *Missouri State Parks* • Right: You can hike to this view of Current River from Bee Bluff on a spur from the Brushy Creek Trail. *Robert Gestel*

A forest researcher called this area "the heart of roughness." This remote, rugged, and scenic setting offers some of the best hiking and backpacking anywhere in Missouri for experienced adventurers.

60 miles of trails
Shannon County

Trails
- Bee Bluff Spur (1.9 mi)
- Blair Creek section of the Ozark Trail (13 mi)
- Blair Creek Equestrian Trail (12 mi)
- Brushy Creek Trail (16 mi)
- Brushy Creek Trail Interior Connector (3.6 mi)
- Current River Trail (5.25 mi)
- Laxton Hollow Connector, to Ozark Trail (2.3 mi)

and full of appeal and adventure for some. In 2014, the L-A-D Foundation donated a lease of the trails in the Backcountry to Missouri State Parks.

Finding these trails is part of the fun. Head south from Salem along Route 19, one of Missouri's original state highways and the first to be designated as an official Scenic Highway. After you pass Current River and Echo Bluff State Parks, you enter the Ozark National Scenic Riverways and cross Sinking Creek. Then turn left on County Road 19-250, which soon turns to gravel as it leads across the Backcountry about twelve miles to the Himont Trailhead. This road is among the prettiest of autumn drives when the colors of the changing oak leaves contrast with the dark green needles of Missouri's native shortleaf pine.

At Himont, you have your choice of trails: east on the Laxton Hollow connector to the Blair Creek section of the Ozark trail, or west on the Brushy Creek loop trail. For just a taste, you can hike out a mile or two and then back.

As the largest contiguous block of wild country in the state, the Backcountry spans thirteen miles east to west and eight miles north to south. It includes three sizable tributaries to the Current River and all of the associated hollows, ridges, bluffs, springs, and caves. The vegetation here reflects the Lower Ozarks with hickory, ash, black gum, shortleaf pine, and a broad array of oak species. A highlight of the native fauna amid these hollows is the American black bear.

About fifty years ago, a newspaper writer from Kansas City hiked through the Brushy Creek area of the Backcountry and returned home to write that it was "the most remote place in all of Missouri." ∗

Harry S Truman Birthplace State Historic Site

1009 Truman St, Lamar

Harry S. Truman was born in a downstairs bedroom of this little house in the county seat and up-and-coming railroad town of Lamar in 1884. *Missouri State Parks* • Furnishings at the home in which Harry Truman was born are appropriate for the period and give visitors a sense of what it might have been like when our thirty-third and only Missouri president was born here. *Denise H. Vaughn*

THE THIRTY-THIRD PRESIDENT of the United States was born May 8, 1884, in a downstairs bedroom of a neat but small frame house in Lamar. The house, purchased for $685, measured only 20-by-28 feet. It had four tiny rooms downstairs and two upstairs, both small and with very low ceilings. It had neither electricity nor indoor plumbing. Set behind it were a smokehouse, a cistern, and, a little distance away, an outdoor privy, typical of the times in rural areas. The house was at the edge of town, and John Truman also owned the property catty-corner across the street. There, he had a corral and barn and traded horses and mules.

Harry S Truman was the first of three children of John and Martha Ellen Truman. His middle initial was a compromise between the names of his grandfathers, Anderson Shipp Truman and Solomon Young. Harry himself used the S both with and without a period.

Lamar was first settled and platted in the 1850s. Wyatt Earp married a local girl and served as the town's first marshal in 1870, but it was not until two rail lines reached Lamar in 1880 and 1881 that its prospects brightened. Even so, when Harry was only eleven months old, his restless young father pulled up stakes and moved his family south of Kansas City, first to Harrisonville, then Belton, and then Grandview.

In 1890, the family moved to Independence, where Harry began school and at age six, first met Elizabeth Virginia (Bess) Wallace, age five. The two were classmates for a long time. Harry fell behind Bess one year when he had diphtheria, but he caught up later by skipping a grade. He was "bookish" rather than an athletic boy, and both he and Bess graduated from the Independence High School in 1901.

There was no money for college, and Harry worked for awhile to help keep his brother and sister in school, and then in 1906, his parents asked him to help farm his Grandmother Young's 600-acre-farm near Grandview. He farmed for eleven years before serving in World War I and then politics.

Throughout his political life, Harry Truman was a strong supporter of organized labor. In appreciation, the United Auto Workers (UAW) of America bought the birthplace at Lamar in 1957 from descendants of Wyatt Earp, had it restored, and donated it to the state in 1959 for preservation. The former president came down from Independence for the dedication on April 19, 1959, along with Gov. James T. Blair, Sen. Stuart Symington, and other dignitaries. "I feel like I've been buried and dug up while I'm still alive," Truman said, "and I'm glad they've done it to me today." He signed the guest book as a "retired farmer."

With no family pieces available from the Trumans' time in Lamar, the house was furnished appropriately for the time of Harry's birth. The period wallpapers, the gingham check cloth on the kitchen table, the rag rugs, and the faint odor of the coal oil lamps successfully evoke the era. A monument to our thirty-third president, erected by the UAW at the time the house was dedicated, stands nearby.

The park division has acquired additional nearby lots, including the site of the mule barn owned by Truman's father, with the hope of protecting the immediate area and reconstructing the barn and also an elementary school that was south of the home.

Meanwhile, the place remains very much as it was when John and Martha Ellen Truman lived there and Harry was born. This plain, small house gives us perhaps the best possible understanding of the extraordinary man who thought of himself as "Mr. Citizen." *

Truman returned to Lamar to accept the nomination as candidate for vice president of the United States as Franklin D. Roosevelt's running mate.

2.5 acres
Barton County

Prescribed burns have restored the natural characteristics of the land, and the park captures the character of both the prairies to the west and the woodlands to the east. Oaks flourish in an open setting and shade a mantle of prairie grasses and wildflowers.

1,440 acres
Benton County

Trails
- Bluff Ridge Trail (2 mi)
- Western Wallflower Trail (0.8 mi)
- 1000th Mile Trail (1 mi)

Harry S Truman State Park

28761 State Park Rd West, Warsaw

THE VISITOR ARRIVING BY CAR meanders for miles along the curvy spine of a narrow ridge. Closer to the park, steep valleys alternating on either side of the road provide nickelodeon glimpses of Truman Lake. A great bend of the Osage River has created a long peninsula so pinched at one point that one can see the lake reaching close on both sides.

Early natives probably hunted Ice Age mastodons and ground sloths here. The famed Rodgers rock shelter south of Warsaw, which revealed some ten thousand years of nearly continuous occupation by Native Americans, has water lapping into it at full pool. Subsequent native people, the Osage, gave their name to the river. A powerful and far-ranging tribe, the Osage played a key role in the early fur trade and exploration conducted by Frenchmen such as Charles du Tisné who led an expedition through the area in 1719. American pioneers began permanent settlement in the 1830s. Much of this region's history and prehistory, plus a good deal of Army Corps of Engineers showmanship, is displayed at the corps visitor center perched atop Kaysinger Bluff.

The corps leased the parkland to the state, and the park, which opened in 1983, is attractive. The park consists of a two-lobed peninsula jutting into the central part of the lake close to Truman Dam in Benton County. Park planners took advantage of a superb location and easily controlled access to create one of Missouri's finest reservoir-based state parks. There are abundant, tidy campsites, clean sand beaches, shady picnic areas, convenient boat launches, and a fully equipped marina. Fishing, sailing, and pleasure boating are all popular, and trails wind through the woods and out to rocky overlooks.

Perhaps because of the park's semi-isolated peninsular setting, wildlife is not threatened and allows close observation. It is not uncommon to see deer, wild turkeys, fox squirrels, and cottontail rabbits feeding along the grassy shoreline near the campground beach. In the winter, numerous bald eagles roost on the tall limestone bluffs bordering the lake.

It is somehow fitting that this superb park, which anchors the reservoir on the Osage River named for the only president from Missouri, should once again exhibit an oak woodland and prairie landscape like the one here when Osage Indians hunted the area or when Harry Truman was born not far from here. *

Top: A shady bluff provides a peaceful view. *Nick Decker* • Middle: A wind surfer catches a breeze. *Scott Myers* • Bottom: Harry S. Truman State Park uses prescribed fire to preserve prairie and savanna landscapes across much of the uplands. *Allison Vaughn*

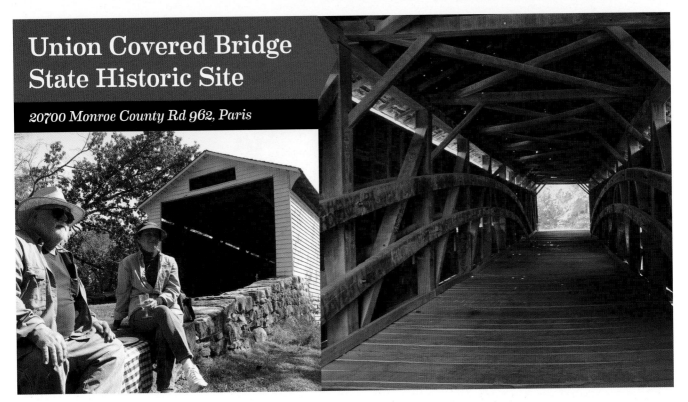

Union Covered Bridge State Historic Site

20700 Monroe County Rd 962, Paris

FOR ALL THEIR ROMANTIC IMAGES, covered bridges were utilitarian. Their roofs provided shelter against the weather, not so much for the convenience of travelers but to protect the wooden structure of the bridge. These bridges proved structurally sound for years, but without the covers, moisture would quickly have rotted the joints where the large timbers intersect. Union Covered Bridge, one of the four remaining covered bridges in Missouri, clearly shows the care and planning that went into its construction.

On September 17, 1871, officials of the Monroe County Court opened the Union Covered Bridge to traffic. The new bridge replaced a dilapidated, uncovered structure spanning the Elk Fork of the Salt River near Union Church, where the Paris-Fayette road crossed the stream. The bridge continued to carry vehicles for almost a hundred years.

Union Covered Bridge was built using a support system called the Burr arch truss. Patented by Theodore Burr of Torringford, Connecticut, the Burr arch truss produced bridges of great structural integrity. In addition to the usual truss made of vertical and diagonal members, Burr's design added wooden arches to each side of the trusses. But Joseph C. Elliott, the bridge builder who had won the contract to build this one, went even further: his bridge also featured double arches on each side.

To form the arches, Elliott fitted multiple timbers, cut from local oak, together with bolts. Then the timbers were sawed on two sides and shaped to the nec-

essary curve with an adze. The careful observer can still see the blade marks left by the builders. Where the large wooden members of the truss connected with each other, the joints were fastened together with wooden pins called treenails or trunnels. Many covered bridges were covered with board-and-batten siding, but the Union bridge sports a slightly dressier siding of clapboards, topped by a wood-shingled roof.

Amazingly, two of Elliott's bridges—Union and Mexico—were still carrying traffic in the 1960s, almost a century later. The active era came to a close for the Union covered bridge when a dump truck with a load of gravel from the nearby quarry partially broke through the bridge floor but, luckily, did not completely destroy the bridge in the process.

The Mexico bridge's end was more catastrophic. On July 9, 1967, a raging flash flood destroyed it. Ironically, the state legislature had just that year authorized the Missouri State Park Board to take ownership and preserve the state's remaining covered bridges, and the Mexico bridge, along with the Union bridge, had been slated for transfer to the park system on July 12. Some of the Mexico bridge timbers were salvaged, however, and used on Union bridge a year later when it was partially restored by state park authorities.

Since acquiring the four remaining bridges in 1967, the state park system restored them all initially, repaired them after repeated flood events, and defended them against vandalism and arson. For nearly half a century, these once utilitarian structures have added beauty and grace to Missouri's state parks. Perhaps they always will, "The good Lord willin' an' the crick don't rise." *

Covered bridges in the nineteenth century were also sometimes known as "kissing bridges" on account of the solitude they offered young lovers. They also provided refuge for weary travelers in need of shade or shelter.

1 acre
Monroe County

Left: Visitors relax and enjoy a picnic on the stone abutments just outside the entryway to Union Covered Bridge. • Right: The bridge is the only one of Missouri's four remaining covered bridges to feature the Burr double-arch truss. *Both Missouri State Parks*

Felix Vallé House
State Historic Site

198 Merchant St, Ste. Genevieve

THE FELIX VALLE HOUSE was recognized as significant by the federal government as early as the 1930s, when architectural drawings of the structure were included in the Historic American Buildings Survey. In 1970 the family home was donated to the state by descendants of the inter-married Vallé and Rozier families. The Rozier family was descended from Ferdinand Rozier, a Frenchman who had arrived in Ste. Genevieve in 1811.

Park officials restored the Felix Vallé house to its original appearance, including reopening the two original front entrances leading to separate sections, and furnished it as it may have been during the 1830s. The house boasts a great expanse of original painted ceiling, protected for more than a century by a plaster ceiling that was placed over it during remodeling around 1850; the newly revealed 1818 paint is covered with thousands of flyspecks, a hint of life before wire screens.

The vertical-log Bauvais-Amoureux and Delassus-Kern houses and other structures are also part of the historic site. They provide a great deal of insight into life in one of Missouri's earliest settlements and into the construction techniques used by the French Colonial settlers. The site is an essential part of any visit to Ste. Genevieve. *

Top: Two front entrances show that Felix and Odile Vallé's home served also as the headquarters for the Menard & Vallé mercantile establishment. *Scott Myers* • Bottom: Built in 1818, the Valle house is furnished in the style of the period with artifacts on display. *Missouri State Parks*

A National Park Service study found that Ste. Genevieve, which has the best collection of French Colonial vertical log houses in the country, merits inclusion in the National Park system.

**12 acres
Ste. Genevieve
County**

Van Meter State Park

32146 N Hwy 122, Miami

APPEARANCES CAN BE DECEPTIVE. A first-time visitor to this park might perceive the place as quiet, maybe even sleepy. Route 122 approaches the park across the broad bottomlands of the Missouri River. The park is part of the steep loess hills—known locally as the Pinnacles—that loom up and border that floodplain, overlooking the river and its valley. At the park, you will see a lovely walnut-shaded picnic ground with two Civilian Conservation Corps-era shelters, a small campground, and an eighteen-acre fishing lake—not a very imposing array. But on a winter afternoon, as you stand on a hill and watch, the sunset washes the bleak and rugged landscape with a persimmon glow. The hills seem to be breathing.

This is also the site of Missouri's American Indian Cultural Center. It explains the cultural history of each of the nine tribes in Missouri in the early nineteenth century: the Osage, Shawnee, Delaware, Ioway, Ilini-Peoria, Kanza, Kickappoo, Sac, and Fox, with a special focus on the Otoe-Missouria. Special programs by each tribe enliven the park.

The first Europeans to touch what is now Missouri are believed to have been Frenchmen—the Jesuit missionary Father Jacques Marquette and the adventurer Louis Jolliet. While exploring the Mississippi River in 1673, they passed the mouth of a great brown behemoth flowing from the west and heard from some friendly Native Americans about a tribe that lived farther up that continent-draining river. Later on, that tribe's name was recorded on their map as Oumessourit, a word meaning "people of the big canoes" in one of several rough interpretations. Oumessourit evolved thereafter into Missouria or Missouri. Thus was the name for a group of people, a great river, and eventually, a state first recorded in a European language.

Archaeologists have made significant discoveries about the Missouria here, including artifacts suggesting they had lived here since about AD 1400 and that both of their sites on the pinnacles and also on the gumbo bottomland supported them well for nearly 400 years. But unlucky alliances with European powers, ravaging European diseases, especially smallpox, and conflict with rivals like the Sac and Fox took their toll.

By 1804 when Lewis and Clark passed by here during their epic expedition upriver, the Missouria village site had been long abandoned. Now, part of their former homeland has been preserved.∗

Top: The landscape includes once typical bottomland marsh. *Matt Faupel* • Middle: University of Missouri archaeology students excavated part of a Missouria village. The site was designated a National Historic Landmark in 1964. *Robert Bray* • Bottom: Missouri's American Indian Cultural Center contains exhibits from nine tribes. *Missouri State Parks*

A site at Van Meter known as the Old Fort was thought to be connected to the Hopewell culture, which dated to the time of Christ. Later archaeologists unearthed artifacts suggesting the Missouria Indians had lived in the area since about AD 1400 and that they had built the fort, although they are no longer certain it was actually a fort or why they built it.

1,105 acres
Saline County

Trails
- Earthworks Trail (1.75 mi)
- Loess Hills Trail (2 mi)
- Memorial Trail (0.4 mi)
- Missouri River Overlook (0.1 mi)
- Oumessourit Wetland Bluff Trail (0.4 mi)
- Oumessourit Wetland Boardwalk Trail (0.5 mi)

Historic Structures
- CCC shelters and camp

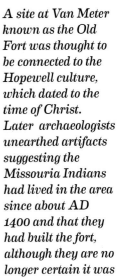

Wakonda State Park

32836 State Park Rd, La Grange

WHAT A PARADOX that in the twentieth century, in an industry-fueled search for gravels, Missourians accidentally created an aquatic playground. Through an unlikely series of events beginning with glaciation during the Pleistocene Epoch and involving intensive human manipulation of the landscape, Wakonda State Park has become one of the state's most enticing recreational parks as well as a refuge for one of its most endangered natural communities: the sand prairie.

The landscape near Wakonda in northeast Missouri was shaped by the southward thrust of massive ice sheets and then by their last retreat when the big thaw set in. The retreat of the glaciers and the melt that ensued caused the Mississippi to carve a broad floodplain along which large, concentrated deposits of gravel and sand that had been carried along by the glacier were left behind. These deposits then lay unremarked until Missourians found a widespread need for them.

After World War I, the increasing popularity of the automobile dictated a rapid improvement in Missouri's roads. A new State Highway Commission set a major mission: "To lift Missouri out of the mud!" The obvious and practical method was to gravel the roads. The search was on for materials, and soon some alert road builder discovered the extensive and easily mined deposits near LaGrange. They turned out to be the best and largest source of road-surfacing material in the state, with about sixteen million tons of gravel shipped from the site between 1930 and 1965.

As a reminder of the deposits' Pleistocene origins, a mastodon tusk and other fossils of the epoch were excavated in the gravel operations. Another indication of their origins was the Lake Superior agate, which demonstrates how far the glacier carried its collection.

Years of dredging scooped out the gravel to deep levels, below the water table in the floodplain, creating lakes. They are clean little lakes because the river water that filled them was filtered through the glacial deposits. The new water bodies soon became popular for fishing and swimming, a perfect location for a park. The idea grew, and on June 5, 1960, the Highway Commission deeded 257 acres on which it had exhausted the gravel deposits to a receptive State Park Board.

Park officials invited suggestions for a name for the new park. Dr. Carl Chapman, a noted archaeologist at the University of Missouri, suggested Wakonda, derived from an Osage and Missouria word meaning "something consecrated." A river north of the site is named Wyaconda.

There are now six lakes, and you may rent a john-

The river water that filled the lakes here is clean because it was filtered through glacial deposits. The park has the largest natural sand beach of any state park, also courtesy of the glaciers. *Missouri State Parks*

boat or kayak on several of them. There are also two campgrounds and numerous picnic sites. Since the lakes are inundated during extreme Mississippi River flooding, they contain many different species of fish. Most anglers target largemouth bass, crappie, bluegill, and catfish, but other species may be taken including muskie, spoonbill, walleye, and northern pike. Attracting thousands of waterfowl during spring and fall migrations, Wakonda is also a destination on Missouri's portion of the Great River Birding Trail.

Mississippi River floods occasionally creep up into Wakonda, but the park continues to attract more than 100,000 visitors a year. In addition to swimming, fishing, birding, and boating, the park offers more than seven miles of hiking and biking trails. Several wind along the lakes and through the sand prairies, where those so inclined can marvel at the natural survivors of a most unnatural history. *

1,054 acres
Lewis County

Trails
- Agate Lake Trail (4.25 mi)
- Campground Trail (0.4 mi)
- Jasper Water Trail (2 mi)
- Quartz Lake Trail (0.3 mi)
- Sand Prairie Trail (1 mi)
- Wakonda Water Trail (3.7 mi)

Wallace State Park

10621 NE Hwy 121, Cameron

ONE OF THE MOST LOVELY FOREST oases of natural land in northwest Missouri is preserved in Wallace State Park near the town of Cameron, not far northeast of Kansas City. You will no doubt be impressed by the fertile farmlands here, but scattered throughout the region are also areas of rough, hilly land, especially near some of the streams.

Wallace was one of the second-generation parks, and only the second to be acquired north of the Missouri River, after Mark Twain State Park. Land was considerably more expensive in north Missouri than in the Ozarks. Its initial 120 acres were purchased in 1932 for a state recreation area from four landowners: 40 acres from W.H. Potter, 40 acres from Grant Siever, 20 acres from the heirs of George Wallace, (brother of William); and 20 acres from William J. Wallace, but only after agreeing that the park be named him. Now about 500 acres, the park includes beautiful forested hills and more than a mile of the valley of Deer Creek.

Visitors will enjoy the beauty and solitude of the natural environment. Rocky Ford Trail follows a gentle downhill slope to Deer Creek. Old Quarry Trail leads you past an old quarry and through a small stand of Scotch and shortleaf pine. Skunk Hollow Trail is a shady path following an intermittent stream. Deer Run Trail takes you through a variety of natural settings. Benches provide resting stops for contemplating nature. Sitting still on these benches is a great way to get a closeup look at wildlife. ∗

The park has a rugged terrain with oaks on the ridge tops, and sumac, dogwood, and redbud in the understory.

502 acres
Clinton County

Trails
- Deer Run Trail (1.75 mi)
- Deer Creek Loop (1.25 mi)
- Old Quarry Trail (1.25 mi)
- Rocky Ford Trail (0.6 mi)
- Skunk Hollow Trail (1.25 mi)

Historic Structures
- WPA roads and picnic area

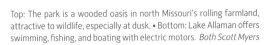
Top: The park is a wooded oasis in north Missouri's rolling farmland, attractive to wildlife, especially at dusk. • Bottom: Lake Allaman offers swimming, fishing, and boating with electric motors. *Both Scott Myers*

Washington State Park

13041 Hwy 104, De Soto

AMERICAN INDIAN ROCK CARVINGS are found in a few other places in the state, including Thousand Hills State Park, but this one park along the Big River contains almost two-thirds of all the petroglyphs discovered in Missouri so far.

The petroglyphs are carved in horizontal slabs of limestone bedrock ledges in the rocky, barren glades of this Ozark Border park. One large group of about two hundred petroglyphs is situated precariously close to Highway 21. Another group of about forty is east of the park's entrance road at the south end of an interpretive building. The third and largest group, numbering some 238, occurs on ledges overlooking Maddin Creek. The petroglyphs depict animals, birds—including dozens of thunderbirds—turkey tracks, snakes, human figures, footprints, hands, arrows, maces, cups, houses, shapes, and other symbols.

The carvings have been known since the first lead miners and farmers arrived in the area. Two groupings have been protected in the park since the first tract was donated to the state in 1932 by A. P. Greensfelder.

The petroglyphs have been analyzed by numerous archaeologists over the years, yet they remain something of a mystery. Although there is abundant evidence of peoples from the Woodland Period and even earlier traditions in the area, archaeologists believe the thunderbirds and other ceremonial symbols are the work of people of the Middle Mississippian culture during the period between AD 1000 and 1600. They seem to relate in some way to the great Cahokia

Washington is the petroglyph park, with three different groups containing almost five hundred carvings depicting animals, thunderbirds, humans, turkey tracks, snakes, arrows, and more.

2,158 acres
Washington County

Trails
- 1,000 Steps Trail (1.5 mi)
- Opossom Track Trail (2.5 mi)
- Rockywood Trail (6 mi)

Historic Structures
- CCC lodge, cabins, interpretive building, office, restrooms, barn, shelters, trails, and stone road culverts

center of Mississippian culture across the river from St. Louis.

The petroglyphs are not the only examples of masterful craftsmanship in stone at Washington State Park. Not long after the land was donated to the state for a park, an African American company of the Civilian Conservation Corps set up camp and began to develop the rugged tract along Big River for recreational use. Inspired by the petroglyphs in the park, the members of the company named their barracks area Camp Thunderbird and titled their camp newspaper the Thunderbird Rumblings. Between 1934 and 1939, these young men, aged eighteen to twenty-five, built many rustic stone structures that blend well with both the rock carvings and the natural rock outcroppings in the park. Among the truly notable features in this park is a lodge, now a park store, constructed of rough random-cut ashlar stone, with a thunderbird symbol carved in the stone facing at the gable end and repeated in interior details such as the handmade iron door hinges.

The park also boasts handsome rental cabins and an octagonal lookout shelter of random-cut native limestone, open on all sides to views of the day use area, bluffs, Big River, and surrounding farmland. Another shelter of native stone resembles a natural outcropping of rock, set into a hillside and offering a spectacular view of the river valley. The 1,000 Steps Trail winds up the hill behind the shelter. The ambitious, labor-intensive construction of these structures blends beautifully into the natural park environment.

The landscape that inspired Native American rock carvers and African American stonemasons still awes visitors and works its magic. *

Left: Celandine poppies grace the 1000 Steps Trail. *Ron Mulliken* • Right: American Indians carved symbols, including animal tracks, snakes, and thunderbirds, in the ancient limestone bedrock. *Missouri State Parks*